THE LITTLE
BLACK BOOK OF

LAS VEGAS

*The Essential Guide
to Sin City*

LARK ELLEN GOULD

MAPS BY DAVID LINDROTH INC.

ILLUSTRATED BY
KERREN BARBAS STECKLER

PETER PAUPER PRESS, INC.
WHITE PLAINS, NEW YORK

THANKS

*My heartfelt thanks goes to Alicia Malone of
the Las Vegas Convention and Visitors Authority,
for her support every step of the way, and to
Bill Becker, who made sure this book
hummed with humor and worth.*

The publisher has made every effort to ensure that the content of this
book was current at time of publication. It's always best, however, to
confirm information before making final travel plans, since telephone
numbers, Web sites, prices, hours of operation, and other facts are
always subject to change. The publisher cannot accept responsibility
for any consequences arising from the use of this book. We value your
feedback and suggestions. Please write to: Editors, Peter Pauper Press,
Inc., 202 Mamaroneck Avenue, Suite 400, White Plains, New York
10601-5376.

Editors: Vicki Fischer, Suzanne Schwalb
Proofreader: JCommunications

Illustrations copyright © 2008 Kerren Barbas Steckler

Maps © 2008 David Lindroth Inc.

Designed by Heather Zschock

THE LITTLE
BLACK BOOK OF
LAS VEGAS

CONTENTS

INTRODUCTION

"Your Vegas is showing." That is, if you're one of the nearly 40 million visitors who stay and play in Vegas each year, testing their mettle on its green felt midways, cruising the neon, and indulging their tastes for fine food, fun, and thrills. Whether you come to get married by Elvis, to ride a space needle 1,000 feet above the Strip, or simply to watch the whirring wheel of fortune, this kaleidoscope of a city allows you to leave your cares behind and surrender to seductions found nowhere else in the world.

The pulsing neon that flashes on as dusk falls represents just a fraction of the energy coursing through this dynamic metropolis. Gaming is the oil that drives this machine; money in measures approaching the GDP tallies of more than a few countries pours into incredible attractions and the never-ending invention (and reinvention) of the city's Next Big Thing.

If it can be dreamed, it can be done—in Las Vegas. At least that's how Benjamin "Bugsy" Siegel saw the future lay of the land when he put a concrete "carpet joint" (slang for an upscale gambling casino) in the middle of the Mojave Desert in 1946.

When Siegel opened the Flamingo, latter-day Las Vegas (Spanish for "The Meadows") sprang from the desert with steel and glass and swimming pools that attracted the Hollywood set. The Flamingo was joined by the

Desert Inn, the Sands, the Riviera, the Dunes, and the Hacienda. The Strip was born. At the same time, Downtown Las Vegas, "Glitter Gulch," was evolving, with the fabled Fremont Street facades of the Golden Nugget, Golden Gate, Binion's Horseshoe, and El Cortez. These two corridors of neon served as drawing cards to what was then dubbed "Sin City."

These were followed by the Aladdin and Caesars Palace; the next wave brought Circus Circus, Imperial Palace, and the original MGM Grand (now Bally's). The 1980s introduced another new phase for the city, with the Mirage and its iconic volcano; from its first eruption of fire, heat, and sound, Las Vegas was never the same . . . again.

Las Vegas visitors should be forewarned: No matter how you've prepared for your time here, expect sensory overload. The neon, the crowds, the mammoth hotels, the outrageous attractions, the heat, the money . . . they all overwhelm. When it happens, slow down. Take a breath. Make a plan. And let this **Little Black Book** guide you through the glitter, the glamour, the marvels, and the madness that is Las Vegas.

HOW TO USE THIS GUIDE:

We have included chapter fold-out maps with color-coded numbers that correspond to the places listed in the text. The **Red** symbols indicate **What to See**,

7

landmarks, arts & entertainment, and things to do with kids. **Blue** symbols indicate **Places to Eat & Drink**: restaurants, bars, and nightlife. Orange symbols show Where to Shop. And **Green** symbols tell **Where to Stay**.

Below are our keys for restaurant and hotel prices:

Restaurants
Price of an appetizer and main course without drinks

($)	Up to $25
($$)	$25-$50
($$$)	$50 and up

Hotels
Price per night

($)	Up to $130
($$)	$130-$250
($$$)	$250 and up

VISITOR INFORMATION

The **Las Vegas Convention and Visitors Authority** *(3150 Paradise Rd., 877-VISIT LV or 877-847-4858, 702-892-0711, www.visitlasvegas.com)* offers a comprehensive Web site and phone numbers for information and resources. **Vegas.com** *(www.vegas.com)* and **Vegas4locals.com** *(www.vegas4locals.com)* also list the latest. You can preview shows and buy tickets online at **Las Vegas Shows** *(800-834-2029, www.lasvegasshows.com)*. Find out what's happening each week in **LVM** *(www.lasvegasmagazine.com)* and **What's On** *(www.whats-on.com)*. Each publication offers coupons and promotions; copies are found in most hotel rooms in town. Visitors may also access **Las Vegas Review-Journal** online *(www.lvrj.com)*; check out listings in the "Neon" section published on Fridays.

LANDING IN LAS VEGAS

McCarran International Airport (LAS) *(5757 Wayne Newton Blvd., 702-261-5211, www.mccarran.com)* supports 42 airlines and over 45 million passengers a year with 96 gates in five terminal arms, including one that is custom-equipped for international flights. Also on hand are more than 50 retail shops and 30 restaurants, snack bars, and lounges. Curbside

checking is available, and the airport is favored with kinder/gentler sidewalk security and faster security lines than other urban airports. However, you will also find intractable baggage tag checkers and long taxi lines upon exiting the terminal. Average **taxi fares** from the airport to Strip hotels run $11 to $15, more than $20 for a trip Downtown. Most hotels have **shuttles** if you don't mind waiting, and curbside shuttles run hotel routes for about

$5.50 plus tip. Families and groups can head to the Strip in a **stretch limo** for $56 plus tip—possibly the fastest way to start your Vegas vacation.

An unusual arrival amenity at McCarran is the **hotel check-in desk**. Some hotels, such as the MGM Mirage and Bally's/Paris/Caesars/Flamingo/Harrah's/Rio have hospitality desks in baggage claim where you can check into your room, pick up your keys, arrange transportation, buy show tickets, and have a hotel shuttle service handle your bags. The MGM desk is open 9AM–11PM; the Harrah's Corp. desk is open until 1AM.

GETTING AROUND LAS VEGAS

The keys to Sin City are simple: The **Las Vegas Strip** runs along Las Vegas Boulevard from south to north, from Mandalay Bay to the Stratosphere. The rest of Las Vegas—residential neighborhoods, strip malls, condos, apartments, and a smattering of hotels and resorts—runs east to west. Interstate **I-15** runs straight through the center of the city, paralleling the Strip, from its origins in southwest California on its course northeast to Salt Lake City. **I-95**, meanwhile, runs east to west from Hoover Dam to the western suburbs and onward to Death Valley.

Although some still consider it a frontier town, Las Vegas is a metropolis of nearly two million souls. Most arrived in the past 15 years, making the area one of the fastest-growing in the U.S. The speedy expansion, however, resulted in over 100 miles of sprawl. Land was cheap, labor plentiful, developers with the right connections were given an easy sign-off, and housing was smart, solid, and downright affordable. But as the city grew, so did traffic. Ill-timed lights, poor planning, crowded byways, and a lack of intelligent public transportation alternatives continue to plague Las Vegas. Buses are slow, crowded, and not recommended for any visitor who wants to get somewhere in a timely fashion. For example, the 2.5-mile ride along Las Vegas Boulevard from the Stratosphere to Mandalay Bay aboard the **Deuce** double-decker bus *(see next page)* takes an average of 69 minutes, according to reports by city agencies. Be prepared to do a lot of walking.

In 2004, the **Las Vegas Monorail** *(702-699-8299, 8AM–5PM M-F, www.lvmonorail.com)* was launched, easing both street and sidewalk congestion along the Strip.

The monorail reaches speeds of up to 50 miles an hour along its route between MGM Grand and the Sahara. Riding the entire length takes about 15 minutes with stops, and provides entertaining views of the backyards of many Strip hotels. Tickets run $5 for one ride, $9 for two rides (shareable), $35 for 10 rides (shareable), $15 for an unlimited one-day pass, and $40 for an unlimited three-day pass, much less than taxi rates. The monorail runs daily from 7AM–2AM (until 3AM on weekends). You can buy tickets online, at any of the monorail stations, and inside the Las Vegas Hilton and Sahara. MGM Grand, Bally's/Paris, Flamingo, Harrah's, Las Vegas Hilton, Sahara, and Las Vegas Convention Center have on-site stops on the monorail line. (Note: Vegas cab company lobbying has prevented the monorail from extending to the airport.)

Free Trams: Between Mandalay Bay and Excalibur, one can take a free tram that also stops at Luxor. Similarly, there is a tram connecting Mirage with Treasure Island. Trams do not connect with the monorail system.

The leisurely **Strip Trolley** *(702-386-7429, www.strip trolley.com)* is another way to get around. It runs between Mandalay Bay and the Stratosphere, stopping in front of major Strip hotels, Fashion Show Mall, Las Vegas Convention Center, and Las Vegas Hilton. A transfer to the service's **Downtown Trolley** allows stops at Las Vegas Premium Outlets, Golden Nugget, Fremont, and Neonopolis, and its **South Loop Trolley** runs from Mandalay Bay to Las Vegas Outlet Center, with a stop at the South Point Hotel and Casino. The rate is a flat

$2.50 per person/per ride (exact change required), or you can buy a one-day pass for $8.00. The trolley runs from 8:30AM to midnight daily, every 15 to 30 minutes.

A double-decker bus called the **Deuce** *(702-228-RIDE [7433], www.rtcsouthernnevada.com/deuce/ or www.thedeucelasvegas.com)* runs around every 7 to 20 minutes, 24/7, between the Downtown Transportation Depot and the Southern Strip Transfer Terminal near South Point Resort & Casino for $1.25 to $2 a ride.

Drivers can take alternate routes when the Strip begins to choke—a phenomenon that occurs daily between 3:30 PM and 8PM, weekends until 1AM. **Koval Lane** runs parallel to the Strip one full block to the east between Tropicana and Sands Avenue. The street marks an efficient way to access MGM Grand, Planet Hollywood, Paris, Flamingo, Imperial Palace, Harrah's, and Venetian without fighting drivers mesmerized by the sights of the Strip or the throngs of pedestrians running to beat the flashing "Don't Walk" light. A segue to **Industrial Road** from the Russell Road exit off I-15 will allow drivers to avoid bumper-to-bumper freeway traffic and run parallel to the Strip all the way to the Downtown area. East/west traffic gets a boost from the **Desert Inn Road** Super Arterial that runs from Paradise Road to Vegas Valley Boulevard in a fast corridor under the Strip, bypassing it and the I-15 freeway.

ALL ABOUT MONEY

Tipping in a town built on luck is an imperative if you are superstitious about money or want good service. A  dollar can buy you a polite smile from a waitress or curb handler, but $5 will bring your car ahead of the rest and ensure your meal arrives before you have to leave to make your Broadway show. A $20 bill will buy you a slightly better seat for that headliner comedian's show. Five hundred dollars will get you out of the line, beyond the velvet rope, and into that "reserved" cabana or front table. When it comes to gaming tables, an equal bet for the dealer by a winning player is always appreciated. Tip a dollar a glass for the free drinks that come your way (but go for name-brand beer rather than watered well-brand drinks, and try to stay sober and alert while your money is in play).

While staying at your **hotel**, use common sense when it comes to services. An outside call made from your room phone means sticker shock at checkout. Expect fees, percentages, and charges added to any room service request (in addition to menu prices), not including the tip for the guy who actually brings you your $20 coffee. Even if you're a hotel guest, health club services will require an entrance fee of $25 to $45. And expect long lines at checkout. Consider upgrading to VIP status; depending on the property, the charge (which may run as little as $15 or as much as $150 per night) provides the benefits of a lounge with complimentary refreshments, VIP desk/concierge services, and a place to go to calm down outside the room itself.

Yes, there still is **free parking** in Vegas. All Strip properties offer free and unlimited parking at all times. Note: At some spots, such as the Golden Nugget, you will need to pay to park if you're not a guest or if you exceed the complimentary time limit. Valet parkers should receive a minimum $2 tip for the return of your car.

STAYING IN THE GAME

If you are going to stay and play in Vegas you might as well know the way in Vegas. When playing the tables or pumping the slots, don't think about winning and losing. Think about the fun you are having and the small (or large) fee you are paying for that privilege. There is nothing like the thrill of the roll. All eyes are on you, and you have chips on hard numbers and more on the come. The dice roll your way, and everybody wins. The excitement is infectious, and you feel on top of the world—you can do anything. Therein lies the magic of Vegas.

To keep the sensation alive and your assets solvent, do not bring more cash than you are prepared to lose. Remember that the house always has the edge, no matter what your IQ or gaming talent. Don't use your ATM card (never use cards in casinos unless you want to incur absurd service fees), credit card, or checkbook. Quit while you're ahead or when the money runs dry, and go

do something else. Take part of your winnings off the table as you play and put it in your pocket or bag so you walk away with something in the end. Don't drink too much while playing. Watch your money at all times—including that bucket of nickels you've been toting. And spread some change around for the dealers and money-changers while you play. It brings luck, and sometimes just the assistance you need.

Do join a **players' club** if you are going to stay and play, and join the clubs that offer memberships valid in multiple resorts and casinos, such as those offered by MGM Mirage, Station Casinos, or Harrah's. That way, points earned at one venue can be cashed at another. It simply requires completing an information application at the players' desk. You'll at least get a logo hat for your time. And if you use the players' card in the machines you play, points add up quickly, can be cashed immediately or saved, and can get you everything from a free buffet dinner to a free Vegas weekend.

MORE TIPS

Table and slot minimums on the Strip tend to be higher than what is required Downtown. Also, **rules and odds** tend to be more in the player's favor Downtown, if the game is what counts and atmosphere/location is secondary. Read the **payoff charts** atop the video poker machines to see if you are getting your money's worth for the wins. Take advantage of the **free lessons** in blackjack, craps, and poker offered in most Strip casinos in the mornings and early afternoons.

Pick one game and learn to play it well. If you enjoy slots or video poker, take advantage of tournaments you can enter without risk at places like Tropicana and Bally's.

VEGAS VERNACULAR

Action—money wagered within a specific period of time. For example, ten bets of $20 each amount to $200 of action. The term "action" typically refers to a wager of any kind.

Active Player—someone who occupies a seat at the table, but is sitting out a hand.

Anchor—the last player to the right of the dealer who is the last to act on the hand before the dealer.

Bad Beat—a tough loss, a sure bet against a dealer's weak hand that is lost to the fluke pull of the right card; or a wagered horse that loses by a nose, after leading all the way.

Banker—the dealer, usually.

Bankroll—the total available chips or money held by the player for the course of the game.

Betting Limit—the set minimum and/or maximum amount of chips that the player can wager on a single bet. The player cannot bet less than the minimum or more than the maximum amount posted.

Black—the most common color used for $100 chips.

Blackjack—an ace and a face card or ten as the initial two cards dealt to a player or pulled by the dealer.

Bust—to go over the total of 21 in the game of Blackjack, thus losing the round.

Card Counting—keeping track of all cards that have been played since the shuffle. Note: This *is* illegal in casinos, which keep an eye out for card-counters and card sharks.

Card Shark—a person who is an expert at cards.

Cashier's Cage—the place in a casino where players go to redeem casino chips or slot receipts for cash. They can also cash checks or arrange credit there. Locals call it "the cage."

Check—a term for a chip in casino gambling. It also refers to the word used by a poker player who does not wish to bet on a round of cards, but wishes to stay in the game with an option to call or raise later in the betting round.

Cold—a term for a player on a losing streak.

Cowboys—Kings or Jacks.

Double Bet—a wager that is twice the amount of the player's usual wager.

Double Down—to double the original bet in Blackjack in exchange for receiving only one more card. To do this, the player turns over his first two cards and places an equal bet alongside the original bet.

Down Card—a card that has been dealt facedown on the Blackjack table.

Due For—term referring to a contestant or team that is considered to be overdue for a win or loss in their next contest or sports event. It could also refer to a losing player who is overdue for a good hand. The "due for" wager is a favorite strategy of many Vegas players.

Edge—the advantage an opponent, or the house, may have in any wager.

Even Money (Blackjack)—when the player takes insurance even while holding a Blackjack. This results in a clear net gain of one bet. Some casinos will allow the player to be paid without actually placing such an insurance bet. This is called "taking even money."

Face Cards—the Jack, Queen, and King of any suit of cards.

Firing—when a player wagers large sums of money, the player is said to be firing.

First Base—the position on the far left of the dealer at the start of each hand at the Blackjack table is considered to be first base, and is the first position dealt during play.

Flat Bet—a bet of the same amount on successive hands.

Get Down—make a wager.

Going Down—losing a wager or series of wagers.

Green—the most common color used for $25 chips.

Grinder—a player who wagers small money.

Hit (Blackjack)—a request by the player for an additional card.

Holding Your Own—neither winning nor losing during a wager or series of wagers—breaking even.

Hole Card—any dealt card which is played facedown on the table.

Hooks—Kings or Jacks.

Hot—a player who is on a winning streak, or a slot machine that is paying out.

House—a term for the establishment that runs a game.

Insurance—a side bet in Blackjack of up to half the original bet, which is offered only when the dealer's up card is an ace. The insurance bet wins double, i.e., 2:1, if the dealer has a blackjack, but loses if the dealer does not.

Juice—can be the "Vig" or house take in a deal or can refer to how much influence a patron has with a resort property in effort to receive favors or upgrades.

Ladies—Queens.

Limit—the maximum wager accepted in the game.

Lock—an easy winner, or a clear no-lose situation.

Natural—a two-card hand of 21 points in Blackjack, or a two-card total of eight or nine in Baccarat.

Nickels—a casino term for chips with a $5 denomination.

Odds—the ratio between the amount to be paid to the winning player and the amount bet.

Paint—Jack, Queen, or King. Picture card. A face card.

Pat Hand—a good Blackjack hand worth at least 17 points. The player, in such cases, is said to have a pat hand and should not take another card.

Press a Bet (Press)—to increase a bet by doubling it.

Pressing—wagering winnings along with the original bet. A player is pressing a bet when he lets winnings ride.

Push—a tie hand between a dealer and a player where no money changes hands. A push in the game of Blackjack occurs when both the player and the dealer have legitimate hands with the same total points. In philosophical terms players rationalize "a push is as good as a win" both on the table and in life.

Quarters—a term for chips of a $25 denomination.

Railbirds—spectators.

Rich Deck—a partial deck that has a disproportionately high percentage of face cards and aces.

Seconds—cheating by dealing the second card instead of the top card.

Settlement—the last stage of any particular bet. Either the dealer takes the player's chips, pays out player winnings, or in the case of a push, exchanges no chips with the player.

Shoe—a plastic or wooden box for holding and dealing multiple decks of cards used in Baccarat and Blackjack. The shoe can hold up to eight decks of cards and is designed to enable a dealer to slide out one card at a time.

Short—underdog. It is often expressed as "the short."

Short Stack—a stack of chips in front of a player that is smaller than the stacks of the other players at the table.

Soft Hand—any hand in Blackjack that contains an Ace counted as 11, without having the value of the hand exceed 21. It is always possible to draw one card to a soft hand without busting.

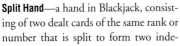
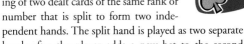

Split Hand—a hand in Blackjack, consisting of two dealt cards of the same rank or number that is split to form two independent hands. The split hand is played as two separate hands after the player adds a new bet to the second hand.

Spread Limit—a betting structure in which a player may bet any amount, within a set range, on every betting round. A typical spread limit structure is $2 to $6, where a player may bet as little as $2 or as much as $6 on every betting round.

Square—an unsophisticated player.

Stand—to refrain from taking another card in Blackjack.

Standoff—a tie in cards between players, or among one or more players and the house. No one wins or loses.

Stiff—a poor hand of cards that is not likely to win.

Surrender—to give up half the value of a bet for the privilege of not playing out a hand of Blackjack. Some hands, such as a 16 against the dealer's 10 or Ace, are so bad that surrender is less costly than playing the hand.

Third Base—the last player to the dealer's right at the Blackjack table. This is often considered a strategic spot because it is possible to see all the hit cards that have been dealt and make a decision on whether the deck is rich or poor in the rank needed.

Under the Gun—the position of the player who acts first on a betting round.

Unit—the dollar amount of a basic bet, i.e., one chip.

Up Card—the first card the Blackjack dealer deals himself that he places faceup for all players to see before they play their hands. The player's decision to draw or stand involves some consideration of the dealer's up card.

Vig—Vig is short for the word "vigorish." It's also referred to as "juice." This can be either the tax the house takes ("the rake") in each hand of poker or the up-front fee.

White Meat—profit.

A FABULOUS WELCOME

The iconic "Welcome to Fabulous Las Vegas Nevada" sign was created 50 years ago by commercial artist Betty Willis at the request of local salesman Ted Rogich, who thought the city needed a unique sign to welcome visitors. Each of the letters in the word "Welcome" is surrounded by a silver dollar, a reference to Nevada's "Silver State" nickname. The 25-foot-tall, diamond-shaped beacon was installed on the Strip in 1959. Ms. Willis never copyrighted the design in order to encourage its use in publicizing the city. The centerpiece of the city's recent centennial celebration, the sign has been called "a powerful combination of symbolism, kitsch, and mythology."

ALL ABOUT THE SHOWS

Once a complimentary amenity in Las Vegas, entertainment is now a revenue generator, along with rooms, dining, and shopping. It's still possible to find a free lounge show for the cost of an overpriced drink or two. But expect to pull out the C-notes for reserved seats at top billers' performances.

And while the headliners still draw crowds, the city's entertainment mainstay is no longer the marquee grabber or retro burlesque review. It's Montreal's **Cirque du Soleil**, which started its run here in a tent behind the Mirage in 1992. The company has launched five (and counting) permanent production shows with custom-built stages for maximum effects: **Mystère** plays at Treasure Island, **O** at Bellagio, **Zumanity** at New York-New York, **KÀ** at MGM Grand, and **LOVE** at Mirage. Expect a new show based on Elvis to open soon within the MGM Mirage complex. Cirque spin-offs like **Le Rêve** at Wynn Las Vegas continue to open.

Meanwhile, **Broadway** is taking a run at Vegas with **Phantom of the Opera** at the Venetian, **The Producers** at Paris, **Spamalot** at Wynn, and **Jersey Boys** at Palazzo. Tickets for other hit New York shows, like **Tony n' Tina's Wedding** at the Rio and **Mamma Mia!** at Mandalay can be found for less than Big Apple box office prices or even the price of tickets for other shows in Las Vegas.

Headliners still rule in lots of casinos and resorts. **Don Rickles** yuks it up at the Golden Nugget, **Barry Manilow** has a home at the Hilton, **Blue Man Group** mesmerizes audiences at the Venetian, **Penn & Teller** pull ironic astonishments at the Rio, and **Bette Midler** has signed on for regular runs in rotation with **Elton John**, **Jerry Seinfeld**, and **Cher** at Caesars.

In addition, you'll find all manner of amusements featuring comedy, magic, hypnosis, music, and mayhem in lounges and stages everywhere in Vegas; hospitality companies rely on these to draw people in so they can see action in their casinos before and after the shows. Ninety-minute choices abound. (Note: Prices listed in this guide do not reflect taxes and "fees" that are tacked on; these vary throughout the city.) Besides going online or waiting on line at hotel desks for tickets, you can look for show kiosks in malls and hotels that allow you to purchase **tickets** up to six hours in advance of the show, if you're not too particular about which production you go for.

VEGAS SEASONS

Rather than asking "when" you should visit Las Vegas, you might ask about **when not to go**. The easy answer: holidays—any holiday. The city is packed on New Year's, most three-day holiday weekends, Memorial Day, July 4th, Labor Day, and school vacations. And then there's Valentine's Day when buffet rooms are awash with white satin.

Midweek is always the **best time** to take on the city. Also, the period between Thanksgiving and just before New Year's seems to thin out a bit. Conventions in town keep the rooms full, but business attendees do not tend to be slot pullers; if there are deals to be found for the leisure visitor, this is the time. Christmas is an interesting time to visit. The Strip is quieter than usual, and the botanical garden at Bellagio is a sight to behold. Most hotels have lavish Christmas trees and lobby decorations (don't miss the Four Seasons Teddy Bear Christmas display), and temperatures are chilly enough outside to make things cozy inside. Some places, like Lake Las Vegas resort, even offer ice-skating on a rink in the desert and steaming hot chocolate at a nearby café.

Most of the year the **weather** cooperates, with moderate afternoon temperatures and sunny skies. Summer is the exception. From mid-May to mid-September, temperatures rise into the high 90s and 100s. Car seats and steering wheels bake, pools crowd, interiors chill (often either too little or too much). Go for early morning tee times and consider whiling away the scorching afternoons in an air-conditioned mall. Keep in mind that it tends to rain during January and July; when it does, it often storms. Flash floods are not uncommon, but a hotel has yet to float away.

SEASONAL EVENTS

Winter–Spring:
Las Vegas Marathon, early December, brings thousands to the streets to party and to run the 26-mile course that winds through the Strip and downtown Vegas; the marathon is one of the 20 oldest in the world. *(702-731-1052, www.lvmarathon.com)*

National Finals Rodeo, mid-December, showcases competitors from all over the world during 10 days of steer wrestling, broncobusting, and calf roping; related events include the Miss Rodeo America pageant, Cowboy Christmas Gift Show, and live entertainment from country and western stars. *(Thomas and Mack Center, University of Nevada, Las Vegas, 702-895-3761, nfr-rodeo.com)*

Ethel M. Chocolate "Light the Night" Spectacular, late November–early January, is when the Mars family of chocolatiers lights up botanical cactus gardens and provides holiday tours of its facility. *(1 Sunset Way, Henderson, 800-471-0352, www.ethelschocolate.com)*

New Year's Eve on the Strip gets partiers and street revelers to pack the entire Strip, so hotels get top-dollar-plus for standard rooms and top name headliners. Note: The Strip closes to traffic, so plan ahead and keep a pair of tennis shoes in your bag. *(702-892-0711)*

New Year's Eve Downtown offers a more orderly, low-key alternative to the Strip celebration, complete with street dancing, excellent live bands, party favors, and fireworks. *(702-678-5777)*

Chinese New Year, February, has celebrations sponsored by the Las Vegas Asian-Pacific Cultural Center throughout the city; this is also considered a very auspicious time to gamble at most casinos— look for lucky tokens, dramatic decorations, and discounts. *(877-VISIT-LV)*

NASCAR Winston Cup UAW Daimler/Chrysler 40, early March, Vegas revs up for this annual event; also watch for the NASCAR Busch Grand National Series and its Sam's Town 300 this month. *(Las Vegas Motor Speedway, 7000 Las Vegas Blvd. N., 800-644-4444, www.lvms.com)*

Clark County Fair and Rodeo, mid-April, is a regional fair featuring livestock, local music, amusement rides, and country cooking about 45 minutes north of Las Vegas. *(Logandale, 888-876-FAIR, www.accessclarkcounty.com)*

Fremont Street Mardi Gras, around the third week of April, features Cajun bands and Crescent City-style celebrating. *(Fremont Street Arcade, 702-678-5777)*

Summer/Fall:

CineVegas, early June, is an international film fest that hosts soirees and nightclub blowouts throughout Vegas in its increasingly successful campaign to become Cannes West; Dennis Hopper is chairman of its creative advisory board. *(Brenden Theatres, Palms Casino Resort, 888-8VEGAS8, or 702-992-7979, www.cinevegas.com)*

World Series of Poker, June–July, is a chance to compete against legendary players (for a $1,000 entry fee) in this million-dollar poker competition. *(Rio, 800-752-9746, www.worldseriesofpoker.com)*

Fourth of July Fireworks features spectacular fireworks from a number of venues. *(Cashman Field, Las Vegas Motor Speedway, Santa Fe Station Pavilion, Desert Breeze Park, Hills Park in Summerlin, Bicentennial Park in*

Boulder City, Morrell Park, Stratosphere Lounge, and Primm Valley Casino); watch from penthouse or roof lounge perches offered by restaurants and hotels around the city.

Professional Bull Rider Championships, late October, showcases top riders and bulls during a four-day competition. *(Thomas and Mack Center, 702-895-3761, 702-632-7580, or 877-632-7400, www.pbrnow.com)*

Throughout the Year:
Rock 'n' Roll Wine Party, monthly, brings revelers together at an ever-changing location for a wine-tasting party complemented by various live bands. To find out all of the specifics, sign up for the newsletter at *www.rocknrollwine.com*

LAS VEGAS
TOP PICKS

TOP PICK!

Las Vegas offers numerous one-of-a-kind attractions and experiences for visitors. Here are 15 of the city's top picks, not to be missed:

★ Fremont Street Experience *(see page 42)*
★ Stratosphere Tower *(see page 61)*
★ Lake of Dreams *(see page 66)*
★ *Star Trek*: The Experience *(see page 67)*
★ Mirage Volcano *(see page 85)*
★ Guggenheim Hermitage Museum *(see page 87)*
★ Forum Shops at Caesars Palace *(see page 90)*
★ Fountains of Bellagio *(see page 91)*
★ Bellagio Conservatory and Botanical Garden *(see page 92)*
★ Atomic Testing Museum *(see page 95)*
★ Liberace Museum *(see page 126)*
★ Red Rock Canyon *(see page 147)*
★ Valley of Fire State Park *(see page 152)*
★ Hoover Dam *(see page 156)*
★ Grand Canyon *(see page 158)*

"Man, I really like Vegas."

—*Elvis Presley*

chapter 1

DOWNTOWN LAS VEGAS

DOWNTOWN LAS VEGAS

What to See:

1. Golden Gate Hotel & Casino
2. El Portal Theater
3. Old Post Office/Federal Building
4. Neon Museum
5. Marriage Bureau
6. Binion's
7. Vegas Vic
53. Golden Nugget
8. El Cortez Hotel
9. Graceland Wedding Chapel
10. FREMONT STREET EXPERIENCE ★
11. Neonopolis
12. Vegas Club's Sports Hall of Fame
13. Plaza Showroom
14. Arts Factory
15. Cashman Center
16. Las Vegas Natural History Museum
17. Lied Discovery Children's Museum
18. Old Las Vegas Mormon State Historic Park

Places to Eat & Drink:

19. Andre's
20. Hugo's Cellar

21. Triple George Grill
22. Second Street Grill
23. Carson Street Café
24. Lillie's Noodle House
25. Pullman Grille
26. Garden Court Buffet
27. Ice House Lounge
28. El Sombrero Café
29. Doña Maria's Tamales
30. Downtown Cocktail Room
31. Griffin
32. Beauty Bar
33. Hennessey's Tavern
34. Sidebar
35. Hogs & Heifers Saloon
36. Jillian's
37. DOME Ultra Sports Lounge
38. Canyon Club
39. Triple Seven Restaurant and Brewery

Where to Shop:

40. Las Vegas Premium Outlets
41. Gambler's General Store
42. Gambler's Book Store
43. Ray's Beaver Bag
44. Funk House
45. Red Rooster Antique Mall
46. Attic
47. Main Street Antiques

★ *Top Picks*

"Most Las Vegans believe
'if it's worth doing,
it's worth overdoing.'"

—John Smith, Las Vegas
Review-Journal *columnist*

DOWNTOWN LAS VEGAS

*The Deuce (bus), operating between the
Downtown Transportation Depot and the South Strip
Transfer Terminal*

● SNAPSHOT ●

History is a rare commodity in Las Vegas, a city where 20-year-old hotels qualify as ancient. But to find flickers of this city's glittering past, one need only to travel to its pulsating Downtown corridor. This is the land of authentic red Naugahyde booths illuminated by buzzing fluorescent lights and attended by gum-chewing wait-resses who call you "honey," of $2.95 steak-and-egg specials (between midnight and dawn, that is), of wooden Indian chiefs guarding magazine/cigar shops, of great lounge acts for the price of a $2 beer, and of gaming rules so loose you can still find dollar tables dealing 21 where you can split sixes, double down on a 2 and a 5 if you want, and watch dealers bust on soft 17. And you can take your winnings to the nearest $5 prime rib special.

Just three miles north of the glamorous Strip, Downtown Vegas carries its own appeal: Its characters come less polished, and its casinos count on hard-core players, rather than romancing couples looking for star-chef dining and bragging-rights rooms. This is Vegas at its grittiest, yet it delivers an honest and satisfying experience to those seeking to be well-treated by hotel staff while they grab their share of Glitter Gulch adventure—for a fraction of what they'd pay on the Strip.

WHAT TO SEE

Downtown Las Vegas has as its epicenter **Fremont Street**, dating back to May 15, 1905, when 110 acres of desert

near the Union Pacific railroad line were auctioned off and a sprinkling of saloons, rooming houses, and gambling halls began to sprout in the arid terrain. When the **Golden Gate Hotel & Casino (1)** *(1 Fremont St., 702-385-1906, www.goldengatecasino.net)* opened in 1906, Las Vegas was on its way to becoming America's adult thrill capital. Today, you can still get a glimpse of that time, from the hotel's smaller, early 20th-century room layouts to its prices: Where else can you down a shrimp cocktail for under a dollar?

Walking east, you'll note the hacienda-style **El Portal Theater (2)** *(310 Fremont St.)*, a 1928 landmark and the city's first air-conditioned building. It now houses a gift shop. Two blocks north is the 1931 **Old Post Office/Federal Building (3)** *(301 Stewart Ave.)*. This Neoclassical building was constructed as part of a government project during the Depression. This was the site of the Kefauver Committee hearings into organized crime in the 1950s. The building has been acquired by the city for use as a cultural facility.

You'll no doubt spy an Elvis or two in the crowd most nights, several ladies of Glitter Gulch in (and out) of outrageous costuming, brides in wedding gowns, large families, and scores of dazed visitors. Water misters cool the air, and all is festive as you walk toward Las Vegas Boulevard and cross over into **Fremont East**, a hip enclave of clubs, cafés, and lofts that is the future of Downtown. Expect a  generous sprinkling of odd shops devoted to jerky, hand-rolled cigars, or cliché souvenirs between the cool and retro neon signs of the nightclubs. Authentic marquees of yesteryear dot the pedestrian walkway. The **Neon Museum (4)** *(702-387-NEON [6366], www.neonmuseum.org)* is actually an open-air collection of restored vintage signs along Fremont Street, including the famous Hacienda Horseman, Aladdin's Lamp, and more. More light-fixture icons are found in the museum's **Neon Boneyard**. Access is by appointment *(call ahead, 702-387-6366)* until the physical museum is built (targeting 2009) and signs are refurbished and electrified once more.

Thinking of tying the knot in Las Vegas? About 120,000 couples a year do. (That's more than 300 nuptials a day, or approximately one every 13 minutes.) First, you'll need a marriage license from the city's **Marriage Bureau (5)** *(201 Clark Ave., 702-671-0600, www.accessclarkcounty.com, open daily 8AM–midnight).*

Bring the right ID (see Web site for requirements, as well as a downloadable application) and $55 in cash. **Tip:** Try to avoid applying for a license on New Year's Eve or Valentine's Day, when lines are out the door and down the street.

To pan Downtown and the lights of the city pulsing across the valley, take the glass elevator up the tower at Binion's (6) *(128 Fremont St., 702-382-1600, www.binions.com)* to the penthouse-level **Steakhouse Bar**. This circa-1951 mainstay is where deals were done over steak and martinis, whether by Vegas mob boss or city manager. The World Series of Poker was born here in 1970 (when the landmark was called Binion's Horseshoe).

Other Downtown icons include old Vegas Vic (7) *(across from the Golden Nugget)*. The 40-foot sign  of a smiling cowboy was installed after WWII and originally had the distinction of puffing smoke and saying, "Howdy, Partner!" He no longer smokes or talks, but his presence draws attention to the **Mermaids Casino** *(32 Fremont St., 702-382-5777)* across the promenade, where you can get deep-fried Twinkies and Oreos for 99 cents. The Golden Nugget (53) *(129 Fremont St., 702-385-7111, www.goldennugget.com)* was built in 1946 and has had nearly nine lives since then, including one with Steve Wynn. It sports an unusual attraction, even for Las

Vegas: a shark tank right in the middle of the swimming pool, which is right in the middle of the hotel, which is right in the middle of  Downtown. Swimmers, separated by glass, can swim with the sharks. Kids can jet through the tank via water-slide with the scary fish gliding around all sides of the see-through tube. The hotel lobby showcases the Nugget's claim to the world's heftiest hunk of yellow on public display—a 61-pound, 11-ounce chunk of gold called the **Hand of Faith**, encased in glass.

Hungry for more of Vegas the way it used to be? Check out **El Cortez Hotel (8)** *(600 Fremont St., 702-385-5200, www.elcortezhotelcasino.com).* Once owned by Bugsy Siegel, the casino has changed little since it opened in 1941, making it the oldest in town. The Fremont Street side still has its original adobe brick, tiled roof, and neon marquee, one of Vegas's most recognizable landmarks. A recent multimillion-dollar facelift transformed a good deal of the interior, but you can still find a steak dinner here for under $5.

No tour of Downtown would be complete without a stop by the historic **Graceland Wedding Chapel (9)** *(619 Las Vegas Blvd. S., 702-382-0091 or 800-824-5732, www.gracelandchapel.com),* where Elvis-themed weddings got their start. The chapel has been featured in films, and celebrities such as Bon Jovi and Billy Ray Cyrus were married here.

The ★**FREMONT STREET EXPERIENCE (10)** *(425 Fremont St., bet. S. Main St. and 4th St., www.vegasexperience.com, nightly, dusk to midnight)* envelops the street with an electric canopy of color and sensation every hour on the hour for about seven minutes. An explosion of digital video presentations runs 90 feet above the pedestrian streetscape on a 1,500-foot-long screen that is the biggest on the planet. The mayor calls it "Viva Vision," and its visual effects and crystal-clear sound system will rock your body. The byway below is lined with kiosks selling gelato, tattoos, fortunes, caps, and souvenirs, and

blues and rock bands perform on stages between shows. After you take in the spectacle, make your way to **Neonopolis (11)** *(450 Fremont St. at 4th St., 702-477-0470, www.neonopolis.com, Su–Th 11AM–7PM, F–Sa 11AM–10PM)* for serious air-conditioning. Catch a new film release here at the 14-theater megaplex, get an ice cream or French roast coffee, or browse the small assortment of novelty shops. Sports buffs will be wowed by the 1905 **Vegas Club's Sports Hall of Fame (12)** *(18 Fremont St., 702-385-1664, www.vegasclubcasino.net, open 24 hours)*. It's one of the world's largest personal collections of sports memorabilia and is available for viewing 24 hours a day. No admission fee. Local hotels host live music and stage performances, ranging from local to name brand. The **Plaza Showroom (13)** *(1 S. Main St., 702-386-2110, www.plazahotelcasino.com)*, for instance, attracts the likes of jazz violinist **Michael Ward**, while comedians such as **Don Rickles** or **Rich Little** frequently take the stage at the Golden Nugget (53) *(129 Fremont St., 702-385-7111, www.golden nugget.com)*. Consult in-room magazines for listings.

While it might be considered a low-rollers' paradise, Downtown has earned kudos for its funkiness by legions of bohemians who've created artist lofts and work spaces flanking the casino area. The **Downtown Arts District** *(loosely bounded by Commerce St., Hoover Ave., 4th St., Las Vegas Blvd. at Charleston and Colorado Ave.)* is coming into its own these days after a good six years in the making. Its draws include antique shops, coffee houses, galleries, and healthy fare cafés. A **First Friday** *(www.first friday-lasvegas.org)* tradition keeps galleries open at night the first Friday of each month; the exhibitions turn into hipster block parties. Another source of downtown entertainment: **ArtAbout**, on the third Saturday of each month *(www.artabout.org, 2PM–10PM)*. The free event features street performers, family-oriented presentations, and regional talent. The center of the district is the Arts Factory (14) *(101–107 E. Charleston Blvd. at Main St., 702-676-1111, www.theartsfactory.com, free admission, hours vary by gallery)*, a warehouse complex of galleries, shops, studios, and arts-related businesses. You can walk in and browse works produced by locals or walk the neighborhood to see fresh interpretations of Las Vegas by the city's emerging talent.

The **Cashman Center (15)** *(850 Las Vegas Blvd. N., 702-386-7100, www.lvcva.com)* is an exhibition arena, with a 1,922-seat state-of-the-art theater, 12 meeting rooms, and a restaurant. It also has a 10,000-seat baseball stadium, which is home to the **Las Vegas 51s** *(www.lv51.com)*, AAA affiliate of the Los Angeles Dodgers. The season runs from April to August, and tickets are usually available at the gate for about $8 to $13.

If you have children and are in search of more traditional museums, try the **Las Vegas Natural History**  **Museum (16)** *(900 Las Vegas Blvd. N. near Washington Ave., 702-384-3466, www.lvnhm.org, daily 9AM–4PM)* for a 3,000-gallon tank featuring sharks, eels, and stingrays; funky dinosaur replications; wildlife and Wild Nevada galleries; and hands-on fun. The **Lied Discovery Children's Museum (17)** *(833 Las Vegas Blvd. N. near Washington Ave., 702-382-KIDS, www.ldcm.org, Tu–F 9AM–4PM, Sa 10AM–5PM, Su noon–5PM, closed M)* is awash with interactive experiences that will keep kids engaged. Children especially love the giant toy train exhibit that allows them to explore the cars' interiors and operate switches, levers, dials, and buttons (complete with realistic sound effects) in the engine car. The **Old Las Vegas Mormon State Historic Park (18)** *(500 E. Washington Ave. at Las Vegas Blvd. N., 702-486-3511, http://parks.nv.gov/olvmf.htm, M–Sa 8AM–4:30PM)*

exhibits remnants of the first permanent non-native set-
tlers in the Las Vegas Valley: Mormon missionaries who
built an adobe fort along Las Vegas Creek in 1855. You
can still see part of the original adobe fort, which now
serves as a visitor center with interpretive displays.

PLACES TO EAT & DRINK
Where to Eat:

Dining Downtown does not have to be over-fried food
and overdone entrées. Although still a haven for inex-
pensive repasts—many of the older establishments
sport their own versions of the gambler's $2.99 mid-
night steak-and-eggs special—the avenues around
Fremont Street are coming into their own as notable
culinary venues.

Andre's (19) ($$$) *(401 S. 6th St., 702-385-5016,
www.andrelv.com/original, 6PM–close, closed Su)* has local,
Michelin-starred chef legend **André Rochat** serving up
such French classics as sautéed filet of beef au poivre and
coquille St. Jacques in a Provence-style cottage home (an
original 1930s railroad cottage with a variety of
French-themed rooms). A world-class wine list is
administered by a resident sommelier. Try for patio
seating if the evening is to be a romantic
one. Reservations required. For a
lavish surf-and-turf menu in a room
with Rat Pack flair, make it **Hugo's
Cellar (20) ($$$)** *(Four Queens, 202
Fremont St., 702-385-4011, www.hugos
cellar.com, daily 5:30PM–11PM)*. This
time-honored gourmet restaurant has

45

been a Downtown favorite for decades. The retro affair includes long-stemmed roses for the ladies upon seating.

The space is cozy and warm, with exposed brick walls and dark furnishings; it draws a crowd, so reserve ahead. Tableside salad preparation and flambé desserts come with the territory. Also worth a mention: **Triple George Grill (21)** **($$)** *(201 N. 3rd St., 1.5 blocks N. of Fremont St., 702-384-2761, www.triplegeorgegrill.com, M–F 11AM–10PM, Sa 4PM–10PM, closed Su)* for steaks, chops, and seafood. This section of Third Street is seeing a revival, with new restaurants and bars in what had been a spot to avoid. The restaurant seeks to re-create the interior of San Francisco's 150-year-old Tadich Grill with a menu of newfangled comfort food bearing smatterings of Italian influence. It's a fun and respectable place for lunch or dinner, with plenty of dark wood accents.

Back on Fremont, **Second Street Grill (22) ($-$$)** *(Fremont Hotel, 200 Fremont St. 702-385-3232, www.fremontcasino.com, Su, M, Th 6PM–10PM, F–Sa 6PM–11PM, closed Tu–W)* is another treasure for those

looking for a gourmet steak-house experience without the usual prices. Its Web site touts what it considers the "perfect introduction to the Second Street experience: a 12-ounce

T-bone steak with all the trimmings for $18.99." Decor is gentlemen's club: oversize leather chairs and dark woods. The menu also sports Pacific Rim choices and seafood dishes. Across the promenade is the **Carson Street Café (23) ($)** *(Golden Nugget, 129 Fremont St., 702-385-7111, www.goldennugget.com)*; the coffee shop is open 24 hours a day and offers an Old World garden experience. Great Monte Cristos and French toast here. For a spot of haute Chinese, dine at **Lillie's Noodle House (24) ($$)** *(Golden Nugget, 129 Fremont St., 702-385-7111, www.goldennugget.com, Su–Th 5PM–midnight, F–Sa 5PM–1AM)*. Formerly the legendary Lily Langtry's, the restaurant serves traditional Cantonese, Szechwan, and Pan-Asian fare in quiet, somewhat exotic/chic surroundings.

At the west edge of Fremont, **Pullman Grille (25) ($$)** *(Main Street Station, 200 N. Main St., 702-387-1896, www.mainstreetcasino.com, W, Th, Su 5PM–10PM, F–Sa 5PM–10:30PM, closed M–Tu)* gets kudos for character. Enter through the original massive doors of the Pullman Mansion and sit near a magnificent oak fireplace and sideboard niche from a Scottish castle. This is the hotel's showpiece dining venue with a menu that features the usual gourmet room offerings of mesquite-smoked beef cuts, seafood specialties, and spectacular desserts at Downtown prices. Enjoy a post-dinner bourbon and cigar in a 1926 Louisa May Alcott Pullman railcar.

Or opt for a simpler experience at the **Garden Court Buffet (26) ($)** *(Main Street Station, 200 N. Main St., 702-387-1896, www.mainstreetcasino.com, daily 7AM–10:30AM, 11AM–3PM, 4PM–10PM)*, the largest buffet in Downtown, with American, Southern, Southwestern, Pacific Rim, Chinese, and Mexican foods, plus designer pizza and pasta, a rotisserie station, and a dessert bar from which to make all-important dining choices. The ambience is fun as well: vaulted ceilings enhanced by Victorian gingerbread decor.

Slightly further afield, the **Ice House Lounge (27) ($)** *(650 S. Main St., 702-315-2570, www.icehouselounge.com, M–F 10AM–2AM, Sa 11AM–2AM)* combines comforting diner fare with postmodern and minimalist design movements and live, funky music. There's some history here—the site was the location of the original ice house that served the entire city. The neon glow outside betrays the electric energy inside with plasma TVs, patio areas, and VIP lounges, complemented by vintage photos on the walls and an aged brick fireplace. Dine on burgers, chili, fries, and sandwiches.

For a casual, south-of-the-border bite, try **El Sombrero Café (28) ($)** *(807 S. Main St., 702-382-9234, M–Sa 11AM–8:30PM)*, a family-run eatery that has been

around since 1950. Enjoy a taste of the sleepy railroad town that once was—with handmade tortillas and enchiladas, served on small plastic-covered tables. Nothing fancy, but if you crave good, cheap Mexican food, this is the place. Another local favorite for lovers of chili and cheese is **Doña Maria's Tamales (29) ($)** *(910 S. Las Vegas Blvd., 702-382-6538, www.donamariatamales.com, M–F 8AM–10PM, Sa–Su 8AM–11PM)*; their tamales are without question the best in town. Locals pack the shiny faux-leather booths during lunch and dinner. Endless chips and ample, well-salted margaritas are a prelude to tamales, served up as red, green, cheese, or sweet. Dinners include generous helpings of Mexican sides with enchiladas, chilies rellenos, burritos, or fajitas. Expect heavy sauces and leave room for Spanish custard, fried ice cream, and squash pie.

Bars & Nightlife:

A new Downtown nightlife is emerging from the dingy pockets of fluorescent-lit souvenir stores, greasy burger joints, and pawn palaces. The **Fremont East** District is dusting off the sidewalks, fancying up the neon, and throwing money at young entrepreneurs willing to invest some creativity and sophistication into the neigh-borhood. From Las Vegas Boulevard to Seventh Street, Fremont is undergoing a renaissance that's attracting hip bars and lounges with its ambience, clublike cafés, and lots of attention from the under-30 crowd.

The entrance of the **Downtown Cocktail Room (30)** *(111 Las Vegas Blvd. S. at Fremont, 702-880-DOWN [3696], www.downtownlv.net, M–F 4PM–close, Sa–Su 7PM–close)* may be its most challenging feature. The club is not marked, and the glass door blends with the exterior until you start pushing randomly. It's an indication of things to come—the bathroom stalls are graced with one-way mirrors. Fortunately, facility users can see out but people at the sink cannot see in. Peruse a stacked martini menu in sleek surrounds livened by popular music tracks soft enough to allow conversations. Just around the corner, the cavernous **Griffin (31)** *(511 Fremont St., 702-382-0577, M–Sa 5PM–close, Su 9PM–close)* is decorated in medieval motifs; a mesmerizing fire pit illuminates its interior. Next door, the **Beauty Bar (32)** *(517 Fremont St., 702-598-1965, www.beautybar.com, M–F happy hour 6PM, M–F 9PM–2AM, Sa 9PM–4AM)* has a lively, kitschy atmosphere right off the set of *Hairspray*. Like the Hollywood original, you can have your martini with a pedicure. Both clubs pack in the crowds on weekends.

Going west, **Hennessey's Tavern (33)** *(425 Fremont St., 702-382-4421, www.hennesseyslasvegas.com, daily 8AM–2AM)*, another Southern California import, is a

rocking Irish pub. This is a great place to sit, have a beer, watch the crowds stroll Fremont, or blend into the weekend club action upstairs at **Brass**. Down the block on happening Third Street, **Sidebar (34)** *(201 N. 3rd St., 702-259-9700, www.sidebarlv.com, M–Th 3PM–midnight, F–Sa 3PM–2AM)* tries to deliver a bit of vintage Vegas in a classy package. Think exposed brick, dark wood, a wine bar, and creative mojitos, with a limited menu of classic appetizers. Park the Harley on the sidewalk and leave the attitude at the door at **Hogs & Heifers Saloon (35)** *(201 N. 3rd St., 702-676-1457, www.hogsandheifers.com, daily 1PM–4AM)*. The bar action is run by the ladies who gave us **Coyote Ugly**, and they rule the show.

Jillian's (36) *(Neonopolis, 450 Fremont St., 702-759-0450, www.jillianslasvegas.com, Su–Th 11AM–11PM, F–Sa 11AM–1AM)* is a poor man's version of souped-up Strip entertainment . . . and that much more fun for it. The huge facility (42,000 square feet) has an ample dance floor for dancing the night away to a line-up of live bands. But you can also watch a game on one of 15 giant-screen TVs, go for bowling and billiards, or try the latest in electronic shoot-'em-ups while munching on American faves such as white chicken chili, steak, burgers, sandwiches, and pizza. A 30-foot "power bar" serves generous cocktails for kindly downtown prices. Never a cover. Get cheapo burgers and beers in a domed perch overlooking the on-street action at **DOME Ultra Sports Lounge (37)** *(Plaza Hotel Casino, 1 Main St. at Fremont, 702-386-2110, www.plazahotelcasino.com, M–F 4PM–midnight, Sa–S 8AM–midnight)*.

51

Just down the street, **Canyon Club (38)** *(Four Queens, 202 Fremont St., 702-387-5175 or 818-879-5016, www.canyonclub.net, Tu–Su 4PM–2AM, closed M)* is an utterly cool, unexpected find. Started by the same folks who launched the **House of Blues**, the room offers touches of that exquisite Indo-gothic decor found in Foundation Room establishments and an unusual roster of bands, such as 1970s blues master Taj Mahal, Eddie Money, the Spazmatics, and Boogie Knights.

Triple Seven Restaurant and Brewery (39) *(Main Street Station, 200 N. Main St., 702-387-1896, www.main streetcasino.com, daily 11AM–7AM)* is the place to go for designer microbrews. Here you'll find five varieties of fresh, handcrafted beers on tap, accompanied by some of the best sports food in the 'hood—pizzas, burgers, pasta, even sushi (this is one of the few places to get fresh sushi Downtown), and it's open day and night. Don't forget to visit the men's room. There's a chunk of the Berlin Wall hanging over the urinal.

WHERE TO SHOP

The savvy staff at the **Las Vegas Convention and Visitors Authority** *(see page 9)* count shopping as one of the prime attractions in Vegas—right up there with ascending the Eiffel Tower, watching the Bellagio fountains, and getting married by Elvis. And Downtown can make a shopaholic's dreams come true—if bargain-priced chain store offerings are of interest. Start

at Las Vegas Premium Outlets (40) *(875 S. Grand Central Pkwy., 702-474-7500, www.premiumoutlets.com)*, with all the big names: **Coach, Jones New York, Bose, Dolce & Gabbana**—more than 120 stores here. When sales are on, the place is jammed. **Fremont Street** itself is fun to browse if you want to buy "Welcome to Fabulous Las Vegas" snow domes, Elvis plates, Mexican jumping beans, jerky, and Harley-Davidson logo items. The  nightly **Fremont Street Experience (10)** spectacle also attracts caravans of odd traders.

Offering items you might not find anywhere else, Gambler's General Store (41) *(800 S. Main St., 702-382-9903, www.gamblersgeneralstore.com)* is a wonderland of casino commerce and as tempting as any department store. This is where you can bolster your slot machine collection and find roulette supplies, Blackjack and Craps gaming tables, chips of myriad designs (including custom-made chips), plus dice jewelry and cards of all fancies. Gambler's Book Store (42) *(630 S. 11th St., 702-382-7555 or 800-522-1777, www.gamblersbook.com)* allows experts to stay on top of the action and novices to get into the action with the foremost collection of gaming literature anywhere on the planet. This unassuming hole-in-the-wall off Charleston Boulevard has stocked the personal libraries of professional gamers for years, offering the latest sheets on seasonal games and a wellspring of

best-kept-secret–style tomes for the card crowd. There are more than 350 books on poker alone—the top category these days, according to the sales staff.

There may not be any grizzlies to shoot around the neighborhood, but after a visit to Ray's Beaver Bag (43) *(2619 Ashby Ave., 702-382-1082)*, about three miles west of the Downtown area, you'll surely be ready if one happens along. This is where to satisfy that musket fixation. Need gunpowder to put in that leather pouch? You'll find it here. Other notions sold at this one-of-a-kind shop: hand-beaded buffalo bladders, handmade American Indian turtle-shell rattles, deer toes and deer claws with which to ward off evil spirits, cast-iron belt buckles, scratch awls, tanned skins, and glass beads.

The **Downtown Arts District** *(along Casino Ctr. Blvd. and Main St.)* is the place to go for vintage clothing, antique furniture, notions, galleries, and crafts stores. The Funk House (44) *(1228 S. Casino Center Blvd., 702-678-6278, www.thefunkhouselasvegas.com)* has an eclectic array of art glass, ceramics, and lighting, and the Red Rooster Antique Mall (45) *(1109 Western Ave., 702-382-5253)* is chock-full of vintage merchandise—from antique farm implements to Depression glass—displayed in individual stalls. Don't forget to drop into the Attic (46) *(1018 S. Main St., 702-388-4088, www.theatticlasvegas.com)* during your foray. This massive vintage clothing store serves somewhat as a hub for the district and is the epicenter of glamour and bargains for shoppers looking to boost their "look" or grab attention with their garb. Find the weird, the wonderful, and the wacky among its stuffed display cabinets and suited mannequins. Wigs, knickknacks, and accessories—especially from the past four decades—abound. Main Street Antiques (47) *(500 S. Main St., 702-382-1882, www.mainstreetantiqueslv. com)* is particularly notable for its warehouse-size rooms of retro oddities and its assemblage of curious collectibles. The owner once operated the Las Vegas Gambling Museum at the Tropicana and displays decades of hotel ashtrays, cups, casino chips, soaps, and cards from Vegas's notorious past. Another spot to seek out is the Rainbow Feather Company (48) *(1036 S. Main St. at Charleston Blvd., 702-598-0988, www.rainbowfeatherco.com).* This Glitter Gulch original is known for its unassuming showroom, shop, and studio, where feathers of all flounces are gathered, dyed, and fashioned into unimaginable headdresses and costumes for Strip production shows. Historic Holsum Bread (49) *(231 W. Charleston Blvd. at S. Commerce St., www.holsumlofts.com)* is an intelligently preserved bakery warehouse packed with decor stores, artists' studios, show galleries, cafés, and exotic notion shops. Shop here for unusual gifts and inspiring art pieces.

WHERE TO STAY

Plaza Hotel and Casino (50) ($) *(1 Main St., 702-386-2110 or 800-634-6575, www.plaza hotelcasino.com)*, at the head of **Fremont Street**, once boasted the best views in Downtown. Now it looks over the firmament of the **Fremont Street Experience (10)** *(see page 42)* but still manages to keep the luster of old Las Vegas aflame. Rooms are basic, and even nonsmoking spaces seem to exude the vestiges of decades of heavy tobacco use, but for the price, lodgings are clean and convenient, and the rooftop pool brings refreshment and views. Next door, **Main Street Station (51) ($)** *(200 N. Main St., 702-387-1896 or 800-713-8933, www.mainstreetcasino.com)* offers a touch of elegance to the Downtown hotel list with simple, graceful rooms featuring gilt-edged mirrors, cream-colored plantation shutters, and tower views over the desert horizon. The casino and lobby area evoke Victoriana with a **collection of antiques** from around the world: chandeliers from the Figaro Opera House in Paris, lighting fixtures from the original Coca-Cola building, and more—brochures located at the front desk provide the key to a self-guided tour. Nearby, the **California Hotel & Casino (52) ($)** *(12 E. Ogden Ave., 702-385-1222 or 800-634-6505, www.thecal.com)* wins big with visitors from Hawaii for some reason, possibly because of its loose slot odds and adults-only policies (you must be 21 to check in and no three-fors in the room). You can have breakfast all night at its **Market Street Café ($)** or take advantage of the $17.99 porterhouse special with salad or soup, a side, and cinnamon-spiced dessert at the retro Vegas-themed **Redwood Bar & Grill ($)**. If there is anything close to "upscale" in Downtown, it's the Golden Nugget (53) ($$-$$$) *(129 E. Fremont St., 702-385-7111 or 800-634-3454, www.goldennugget.com)*. Dating from 1946, the property recently received a $170 million re-do and now boasts a humongous shark and exotic fish aquarium and a three-story enclosed water-slide at pool center, as well as the only luxury spa and loaded sushi bar in the 'hood. It's had the AAA Four Diamond rating for nearly 30 years—the longest winning streak in Nevada history. Four Queens Hotel & Casino (54) ($) *(202 Fremont St., 702-385-4011 or 800-634-6045, www.fourqueens.com)* is a Downtown institution, having occupied its three-plus acres spot since 1966. Here's the place to chance a pull on the **world's largest slot machine** *(just inside the Fremont St. entrance)*. Rooms are plain but large. Do not expect frills of any sort. The stuffiness, lack of views, and fluorescent lighting throughout keep accommodations in the "budget" section of choices. However, for visitors more concerned with happenings outside their rooms, the Queens' quarters will do just fine. Here, too, is one of the few cigar bars Downtown; buy a stogie and smoke it in the corner of the **Chicago Brewing Company ($)**, slightly removed from the madding casino crowd. Five hand-hewn microbrews are on tap, as well as a home-brewed root beer, mini pizzas, fried calamari, and other mouth-watering munchies.

chapter 2

NORTH STRIP

NORTH STRIP

What to See:
1. STRATOSPHERE TOWER ★
2. Thrill Rides—Big Shot, X Scream, and Insanity
3. *American Superstars*
4. Bite
5. Speed—The Ride
6. Amazing Johnathan
7. Musical History of the King
8. Scintas
9. Circus Circus
10. *An Evening at La Cage*
11. *Crazy Girls*
12. *Ice*
13. LAKE OF DREAMS ★
14. *Spamalot*
15. *Le Rêve*
16. Barry Manilow
17. *STAR TREK*: THE EXPERIENCE ★
18. *Rat Pack Is Back*
19. Las Vegas Convention Center

Places to Eat & Drink:
20. Top of the World
21. Luv-It Frozen Custard
22. House of Lords Steak House

★ *Top Picks*

23. NASCAR Café
24. THE Steak House
25. Alex
26. Daniel Boulud Brasserie
27. Bartolotta Ristorante di Mare
28. Café Ba-Ba-Reeba
29. The Capital Grille
30. Capriotti's
31. Café Heidelberg German Deli & Restaurant
32. Polly Esthers
33. Romance Lounge
34. Peppermill Fireside Lounge
35. Blush
36. Tryst
37. Tempo

Where to Shop:
38. Tower Shops
39. Esplanade
40. Fashion Show Mall
41. Bonanza Gift Shop
42. Don Pablo Cigar Company

Where to Stay:
43. Stratosphere
44. Sahara
45. Wynn Las Vegas
46. Las Vegas Hilton

NORTH STRIP

*Monorail stops: Sahara, Las Vegas Hilton,
Las Vegas Convention Center*

• SNAPSHOT •

The North Strip had been the shut-out second cousin of
the glitzy Las Vegas Strip . . . that is,
until Steve Wynn transformed the
aging Desert Inn into the sleek
bronze monolith bearing his name
at 3131 Las Vegas Boulevard South.
Now the center of the Strip is
edging into the North's former
wasteland of strip malls, hangers-on
casinos, and hokey attractions that make up a hodge-
podge link to Downtown. Donald Trump is building
two golden high-rises across the way from the New
Frontier. And the New Frontier is destined for the land
beyond, as plans are in process for its closure and implo-
sion, making way for a 3,500-room, New York
Plaza–themed luxury property to open in 2011. The old
Stardust nearby bit the dust in 2006; now the backhoes
are busy creating mammoth Echelon Place here. Set to
open in 2010, the project, covering 87 acres, will
include five towers, joining MGM Mirage CityCenter
in a new trend of all-inclusive "pods" built to ensure that
guests never need leave the vicinity of their accommodations.

North Strip transition will continue as its real estate values edge into the stratosphere (as well as toward the Stratosphere Hotel), with prices exceeding $30 million an acre. If you're looking for the vintage Vegas of the '60s and '70s, you can still catch glimpses of it along the stretch from the Stratosphere to the Wynn. The Sahara (circa 1952), the Riviera (circa 1955), Circus Circus (circa 1968), the Peppermill, Slots-A-Fun, and assorted souvenir, sandwich, and sexy lingerie spots salt this strand of boulevard, making fun retro discoveries possible, even with the rumble of construction in the distance.

WHAT TO SEE

Why not start at the top? Double-decker elevators fly up the 101 stories in 30 seconds and offer the best vantages in Vegas from the 1,149-foot ★STRATOSPHERE

TOP PICK!

TOWER (1) *(Stratosphere, 2000 Las Vegas Blvd. S., closest monorail stop: Sahara, 702-380-7777, www.stratosphere hotel.com/observation_deck.html, Su–Th 10AM–1AM, F–Sa 10AM–2AM)*. The tallest building west of the Mississippi, the tower offers indoor and outdoor observation decks and breathtaking 360-degree views. But most people opt for the adrenaline-laced view that can be had one level up, outside, and over the railing, as you wait for a turn on one of a trio of the world's highest **Thrill Rides—Big Shot, X Scream, and Insanity (2)** *(Stratosphere, 2000 Las Vegas Blvd. S., closest monorail stop: Sahara, 702-380-7777, www.stratosphere.com, Su–Th*

10AM–1AM, F–Sa 10AM–2AM). The ticket for the elevator ride alone is $10.95 ($7 for children). But rates can be bundled with rides for a discount. Single rides cost $9. On top of the tower, a young, wired crowd queues around the wind-whipped outer rim of the needle for turns at **Big Shot**, which zips them 160 feet in the air at 45 miles per hour to a vantage 1,081 feet up, then back down again for four gut-wrenching Gs, legs dangling over the Las Vegas skyline. Or else they're awaiting **Insanity**—an opportunity to hang 64 feet over the edge of the tower and spin around at speeds that provide up to three Gs, while inching toward an angle of 70 degrees 900 feet above the sidewalk. Or they're going for **X-Scream**, a massive teeter-totter 866 feet in the air, where they'll be propelled headfirst 27 feet over the edge of the tower; here, they dangle weightlessly above the Strip before being pulled back. Repeat. Those with acrophobia might as well head for the casino-level shopping or the swimming/Euro-bathing scene poolside.

Early-evening entertainment here includes *American Superstars* (3) *(Stratosphere, 2000 Las Vegas Blvd. S., closest monorail stop: Sahara, box office 702-380-7711, www.stratospherehotel.com, Su–Tu 7PM, W, F, Sa 6:30PM and 8:30PM, dark Th)*, a celeb tribute featuring "Britney Spears," "Michael Jackson," "Madonna," and "Elvis." Tickets start at $30.95. Adults-only erotic adventure **Bite (4)** *(Stratosphere, 2000 Las Vegas Blvd. S., closest*

monorail stop: Sahara, 702-380-7711, www.stratosphere hotel.com, 10:30PM, dark Th) features vampires who slither through the night topless. Admission is $45.95.

North Strip fun continues with **Speed—The Ride (5)** *(Sahara, 2535 Las Vegas Blvd. S., monorail stop: Sahara, www.saharavegas.com/NASCAR/SPEED-facts; single ride $10, all-day pass $21.95, Su–Th 10AM–11PM, F–Sa 11AM–1AM, times may vary summers and holidays)* at the venerable **Sahara (44)**. The ride revs from 0 to 70 mph in seconds as it whips out of the hotel and up the marquee to an altitude of 224 feet, and back down again for thrills in reverse. The hotel also boasts a 35,000-square-foot **Cyber Speedway** (with race car simulators seven-eighths the size of actual stock and Indy cars), a **PitPass Arcade**, and a **NASCAR RaceWear** boutique.

The stages at **Sahara (44)** have hosted the likes of the Beatles, Frank Sinatra, Dean Martin, Jerry Lewis, Johnny Carson, and Tina Turner. While the current marquee does not blaze headliners, it is possible to see latter-day versions of the Drifters, Coasters, and Platters (nightly 7:30PM) for $47.15 a ticket. If potty-mouthed magicians with a comedic edge are more to your liking, take in **Amazing Johnathan (6)** *(Sahara, 2535 Las Vegas Blvd. S., box office: 702-737-2515, monorail stop: Sahara,* *www.saharavegas.com, F–Tu 10PM, tickets start at $57.45).* Trent Carlini does some of the best Elvis in town in the **Musical History of the King (7)** *(Sahara, 2535 Las Vegas Blvd. S., monorail stop: Sahara, box office 702-737-2515, www.saharavegas.com, M–Sa 9PM, tickets start at $49).* And the **Scintas (8)** *(Sahara, 2535 Las Vegas Blvd. S., monorail stop: Sahara, box office 702-737-2515, www.saharavegas.com, M–Sa 7PM),* a talented musical family combines comedy, song, sound, and impersonations. Tickets start at $49.

Other sky-high attractions can be found under the Big Top at **Circus Circus (9)** *(2880 Las Vegas Blvd. S., closest monorail stop: Sahara, 702-734-0410, www.circuscircus. com).* The 1968 property marked a dramatic shift in Las Vegas concepting from adults-only playground to family playland. The property was also the first truly themed mega-hotel built on the Strip, setting off a fantasy-property building spree that continues to this day. Warning: The foot-traffic chaos of a hotel designed to handle volumes of 40 years ago can be daunting.

Now, as then, gamblers and guests are treated to a **three-ring circus** at casino level with highly-skilled performers, from animal taming to clown stunts to trapeze flights to aerial and contortion maneuvers *(hourly from 11AM–midnight for 10–20 minute sessions).* A crowded midway (featured in the 1971 James Bond film *Diamonds Are*

Forever) overlooks casino and circus arenas. To the rear of the property is the five-acre **Adventure Dome Theme Park** *(www.adventuredome.com, open 10AM–9PM or midnight, depending on time of year)*, an air-conditioned  dome containing some 16 rides, from corkscrew coasters to carousels—often the perfect answer to the question of where to send the brood when private or gaming time is needed. All-day passes with unlimited rides run $24.95 for adults, $14.95 for kids, or $4 to $7 a ride.

Across the street, at 1960s Strip institution **The Riviera**, *An Evening at La Cage* **(10)** *(Riviera, 901 Las Vegas Blvd. S., monorail stop: Las Vegas Hilton, box office: 702-794-9433, www.rivierahotel.com, W–M 7:30PM)* has been pulling in crowds for nearly two decades with a side-stitching line-up of female celebrity impersonators; the memorable Frank Marino is at the helm as an impossible Joan Rivers. Tickets are $55. *Crazy Girls* **(11)** *(Riviera, 901 Las Vegas Blvd. S., monorail stop: Las Vegas Hilton, box office: 702-794-9433, www.rivierahotel.com, every night but Tu 9:30PM)* is an adults' only review, featuring something from all fronts, so to speak: beauty, sex, music, dance and song, and comedy. Tickets are $34.95. **Le Bistro Theatre** here runs a revolving schedule of performances including a Neil Diamond sing-alike, demented hypnotist Dr. Scott, and the Barbra Streisand/Frank Sinatra look-and-sound-alike show called "The Concert That Never Was." Prices and times vary. *Ice* **(12)** *(Riviera, 901 Las Vegas Blvd. S., monorail*

stop: Las Vegas Hilton, box office: 702-794-9433, www.rivierahotel.com, nightly 8PM, dark F) is the show to see if you like skating, Russian ballet, and circus feats. Some 42 star athletes from Moscow work the frozen stage with award-winning movements and choreography. Tickets start at $59.95.

Steve Wynn is known for his crowd-pleasing attractions, such as the erupting **volcano** fronting the **Mirage** *(see page 85).* But the Vegas mogul placed his most recent signature attraction inside his new hotel: the ★**LAKE OF DREAMS (13)** *(Wynn Las Vegas, 3131 Las Vegas Blvd. S., monorail stop: Las Vegas Convention Center via Wynn shuttle, 800-288-7206 or 702-733-4300, www.wynnlasvegas.com, shows approximately every half hour after dark).* Shows center around an ethereal lake with a 90-foot waterfall cascading off a "mountain" covered with 1,500 fir trees. Images from over 4,000 lights are projected onto the falls and lake and set to music, and a screen rises over the mountain; the program combines plot-driven puppetry (including a 24-foot "muse's head"), sculpture, imagery, and dance. Premier viewing goes to those seated for drinks at **Parasol Up** or **Parasol Down**, or for dinner at **Daniel Boulud Brasserie** or **SW Steakhouse**. Those opting to stand must fight for viewing space in a narrow, lobby-level corridor.

TOP PICK!

Your quest for comedy ends with hilarious Broadway hit *Spamalot* **(14)** *(Wynn Las Vegas, 3131 Las Vegas Blvd. S., monorail stop: Las Vegas Convention Center via Wynn* shuttle, 800-288-7206 or 702-733-4300, www.wynn lasvegas.com, Su–W, F 8PM, Sa 7PM and 10PM, dark Th).

The Monty Python spin-off about King Arthur, his knights, and their search for the Holy Grail keeps audiences in stitches at varying times and for ticket prices starting at $69. **Le Rêve (15)** (Wynn Las Vegas, 3131

Las Vegas Blvd. S., monorail stop: Las Vegas Convention Center via Wynn shuttle, box office: 702-770-9966, www.wynnlasvegas.com, M, Th, Su 7PM and 9:30PM; F 8:30PM, Sa 8PM and 10:30PM; dark Tu, W), French for "The Dream," is a hotel exclusive. Artful acrobatics play out on a liquid stage in an intimate theater-in-the-round. The show was designed by Franco Dragone, Cirque du Soleil's former creative director. Tickets start at $99.

The **Las Vegas Hilton (46)** hosts the one and only **Barry Manilow (16)** (Las Vegas Hilton, 3000 Paradise Rd., monorail stop: Las Vegas Hilton, box office: 702-732-5755, www.lvhilton.com), singing "Mandy" and "Copa" most nights at 8PM for prices starting at $95. You may also boldly go to the hotel's popular ★**STAR TREK**: THE EXPERIENCE **(17)** (Las Vegas Hilton, 3000 Paradise Rd., monorail stop: Las Vegas Hilton, 888-GO-BOLDLY

TOP PICK!

[462-6535], www.startrekexp.com, shops open at 11AM, ticket desk at 11:30AM, rides at noon). Its **Museum of the Future** houses the largest collection of *Star Trek* "stuff" outside Hollywood's studio warehouses.

See glass-encased Borg mannequins in full costume (and Borg drones wandering the admission lines) and all manner of models, weapons, clothing, and props used in the four television series and nine films. This space-age attraction offers two multimillion-dollar multimedia experiences. First, get beamed aboard the Starship *Enterprise* during **Klingon Encounter**. When something goes "terribly wrong" and the ship is attacked, you're whisked to an immersive, interactive mission aboard a motion simulator. Ultimately, you return to Las Vegas today (as evidenced by a 21st-century TV "newscast" and low-tech janitorial closet with mop at the exit). Second, you'll find resistance to **Borg Invasion in 4D** futile. Here, the Borg Collective is coming to assimilate . . . can you escape? Flee through an industrial-looking spaceship set, then watch a 3-D film of your getaway while experiencing sensory surprises in your seat, via 23,000 watts of 12-channel sound and special effects. Each attraction lasts about 20 minutes. Dual mission tickets are pricey—$42.99 per person—but your hand stamp lets you get back in line. Afterward, quaff a "Cardassian Cooler" or share a "Warp Core Breach" at **Quark's Bar & Restaurant ($-$$)** *(call 702-697-8725 for reservations)*. Trek-themed eats ("HamBorgers," "Sulu Toss"), desserts ("Deanna Troi's Chocolate Obsession"), and coffees are available, too ("LaForge's Latte," anyone?). Retail therapy awaits at the **Deep Space Nine Shopping Promenade**. You can even have a ***Star Trek*** wedding—call 702-697-8750 for out-of-this-world nuptial ideas.

Can't do Vegas without a dose of Dean Martin or Sammy Davis, Jr.? The *Rat Pack Is Back* (18) plays at the **Greek Isles** *(305 Convention Center Dr., monorail stop: Las Vegas Convention Center, box office: 702-737-5340, www.greekislesvegas.com, Sa–Th 7PM)*. Dino, Sammy, Frank, and Joey, cocktails in hand, come with or without dinner, depending on whether you choose the 5:30PM dinner seating (a rare option in Vegas these days) for $71, or general admission for $57.

Many Vegas visitors (including you?) are in town to attend meetings and trade shows at the sprawling 3.2-million-square-foot **Las Vegas Convention Center (19)** *(3150 Paradise Rd., monorail stop: Las Vegas Convention Center, 702-892-0711, www.lvcva.com)*.

PLACES TO EAT & DRINK
Where to Eat:

Vegas is mostly about "where to eat" rather than "what to eat." And *where* usually depends on your wallet. There are buffets for all price ranges and tastes, as well as coffee shops, gourmet rooms, spaces with views, kitchens with star power, and hidden cafés off the tourist trail. Hotels consider this amenity a convenience and have made an art of providing for every culinary interest and budget. But getting around Las Vegas can be tricky. There is the heat to consider, and there are valet exchanges, parking rounds, traffic jams, and crowded sidewalks. Plan ahead and dine where you intend to be at mealtime. And plan to have lots of time and patience—for getting to and finding the venue of choice and for coping with long lines and overwhelmed staff. If reservations are an option, make them. If a VIP buffet pass through the casino players' points desk is a possibility, take it. If dining early or late can fit into your plans, do it. The 40 million visitors that flock here annually all want to eat, and that can mean lengthy, slow-moving lines even in a city skilled in crowd management.

The **Stratosphere (43)** offers the most memorable dining option—a truly fine gourmet meal in a revolving room 1,000 feet above the city. At its **Top of the World ($$$) (20)** (*Stratosphere, 106th floor, 2000 Las Vegas Blvd. S., closest monorail stop: Sahara, 702-380-7711, daily 11AM–3PM, 5:30PM–11PM*), diners get a complimentary trip to the top and enjoy generous portions of prime rib, rack of lamb, and other high-ticket entrées, accompanied by an excellent wine list.

One light north of the 'Sphere, join the locals in the walk-up window line for **Luv-It Frozen Custard (21)** (*505 E. Oakey Blvd., 702-384-6452, www.luvitfrozencustard. com, T, W, Th 1PM–10PM, F–Sa 1PM–11PM, closed Su–M, cash only*). Try the Western sundae, with hot caramel, hot fudge, and salted pecans. Other crowd-pleasers: chocolate-covered frozen bananas, Luv Sticks (frozen custard bars), and root beer floats.

The **Sahara (44)** may have the last 1960s-style gourmet room in the city. **House of Lords Steak House ($$$) (22)**

(Sahara, 2535 Las Vegas Blvd. S., monorail stop: Sahara, 702-737-2111, www.saharavegas.com, M–F 5PM–10PM, Sa–Su 5PM–11PM) was the place to be seen back in the day when Joey Bishop, Buddy Hackett, Frank Sinatra and friends dined there. It's still an elegant, intimate setting with waterfalls, plush seating, and hovering waiters serving New York strip steaks, Australian lobster tails, lamb chops with rosemary mint glaze, and beef Oscar. Cap off your meal with the restaurant's legendary hot-pear bread pudding or classic cheesecake. At the other end of the spectrum, the hotel's **NASCAR Café ($) (23)** *(Sahara, 2535 Las Vegas Blvd. S., monorail stop: Sahara, 702-737-2111, www.saharavegas.com, M–Th 11AM–10PM, F 11AM–11PM, Sa 10AM–midnight, Su 9AM–10PM)* packs in racing fans with its decor, which boasts nearly 20 authentic NASCAR stock cars—including the world's largest Pontiac Grand Prix stock car weighing in at more than three tons—and other memorabilia on two levels. Big-screen TVs with state-of-the-art sound bring the track to the table. The crowd-pleasing menu includes burgers, steaks, ribs, barbecue chicken, Buffalo wings, pasta, and pizza.

Circus Circus (9) offers bargain dining as well as buffets. **THE Steak House ($-$$) (24)** *(2880 Las Vegas Blvd. S., 702-734-0410, www.circuscircus.com, 7AM–10PM)* serves ample platefuls of aged mesquite-grilled steaks and well-shaken martinis in an atmosphere evoking a British hunting lodge. The hotel's **Circus Buffet** *(7AM–10PM)*,

one of the largest in Las Vegas, is also one of the cheapest ($11.99 for dinner).

Wynn Las Vegas (45) *(3131 Las Vegas Blvd. S., monorail stop: Las Vegas Convention Center via Wynn shuttle, 702-284-DINE or 888-352-DINE, www.wynn lasvegas.com)* has some 18 dining establishments, most offering sumptuous settings equal to the food. At **Alex ($$$) (25)** *(Th–Tu 6PM–10PM),* **Alessandro Stratta**, a James Beard award winner and Mobil Five-Star cuisinier, brings the flavor of the French Riviera to Vegas with superb tasting menus starting at $195. At **Daniel Boulud Brasserie ($$$) (26)** *(5:30PM–10:30PM),* for instance, watch the Lake of Dreams (13) sequences unfold from some of the best seats in the house between bites of the famed DB Burger—nine ounces of sirloin topped with braised short ribs and black truffles with a parmesan bun and true French fries. **Bartolotta Ristorante di Mare ($$$) (27)** *(5:30PM–10:30PM)* serves fresh seafood flown in daily from Mediterranean markets, plus pastas and Italian specialties. Chef Paul Bartolotta's menu includes everything from Ligurian octopus salad to charcoal-grilled Sicilian amberjack to *tartufi bianchi*—white Italian truffles—"the food of gods and kings."

Across the street at Fashion Show Mall (40), **Café Ba-Ba-Reeba ($) (28)** *(3200 Las Vegas Blvd. S., 702-650-5186, www.cafebabareeba.com, lunch Sa–Su 11:30AM–4PM,* dinner *Su–Th 4PM–11PM, F–Sa 4PM–midnight, happy hour M–F 4PM–7PM)* is the spot for tapas and paella. Outdoor seating overlooks the Strip (and is cooled by misters in summer). Yes, that cowboy rib-eye is on the menu, but the roasted eggplant with goat cheese or Spanish artisanal cheese samples, paired with a glass of chilled sangria, is the recommended way to go. **The Capital Grille ($$$) (29)** *(Fashion Show Mall, 3rd level, 3200 Las Vegas Blvd. S., 702-932-6631, www.thecapital grille.com, lunch M–F 11:30AM–4PM, Sa noon–4PM, dinner M–Sa 4PM–10:30PM, Su 4PM–10PM)* is a convenient place for steaks and seafood, should time and expense accounts need to be spent. Three-martini power meals are the norm here, and the service meets the quality of the meal.

Capriotti's ($) (30) *(324 W. Sahara Ave., 702-474-0229, www.capriottis.com, M–F 10AM–5PM, Sa 11AM–5PM)* serves up great deals on huge subs. Try the Bobby— Thanksgiving dinner on a bun—or Slaw B Joe—roast beef, coleslaw, and Russian dressing. **Café Heidelberg German Deli & Restaurant ($-$$) (31)** *(610 E. Sahara Ave #2, 702-731-5310, daily 10AM–9PM)*, an atypical Bavarian-style Vegas eatery (try the sausage sampler), is usually filled with locals. Fans of Teutonic wines and beers will find Vegas's largest selection here, plus live entertainment on weekends.

Bars & Nightlife:

Most Strip resorts have lounges where, for the price of one or two costly drinks, you can watch a band belt out popular tunes. But some bars stand out from the crowd

for their ambient twists. You'll find two such spots at the **Stratosphere (43)**: Polly Esthers (32) *(Stratosphere, 2000 Las Vegas Blvd. S., closest monorail stop: Sahara, 2000 Las Vegas Blvd. S., 702-889-1989, www.pollyestherslv.com, open M, W–Sa 10PM–4AM)* offers four club rooms, each decked out for a different era: '70s, '80s, '90s, and 2000. Dance to the music of each decade, check out cultural artifacts on exhibit, and indulge in themed drinks like the '70s-style "Seamonkey," "Jaws," and the "Godfather." And if lights and heights have anything to do with it, sky-high **Romance Lounge (33)** *(Stratosphere, 2000 Las Vegas Blvd. S., closest monorail stop: Sahara, 888-236-7495 or 702-380-7777, www.stratosphere.com, Su–Th 4PM–1AM, F–Sa 4PM–2AM)* is as intimate as it gets. Enjoy the jazz combo.

Peppermill Fireside Lounge (34) *(2985 Las Vegas Blvd. S., 702-735-7635, www.peppermilllasvegas.com, open 24 hours)* is a favorite local spot with all the retro Vegas one could wish for in a cocktail context. Fishbowls of multi-colored tiki drinks overflow with straws and paper parasols. Slip into one of these bombers while sitting on a comfy couch and watch the centerpiece volcano erupt in a Jacuzzi-sized pool of flames. Truly Vegas.

Blush (35) *(Wynn Las Vegas, 3131 Las Vegas Blvd. S., monorail stop: Las Vegas Convention Center via Wynn shuttle, 702-770-3633, www.wynnlasvegas.com, open* *nightly at 9PM)*, a new casino-level boutique nightclub, morphs from chic lounge to late-night club. Dress code prohibits athletic wear, oversized jeans, baggies, or hats. **Tryst (36)** *(Wynn Las Vegas, 3131 Las Vegas Blvd. S., monorail stop: Las Vegas Convention Center via Wynn shuttle, 702-770-3375, www.wynnlasvegas.com, Th–Su 10PM–4AM)* is the hotel's pulsating club component—a 12,000-square-foot space with dancing, bottle service, and "beautiful people" who come to be seen and experience the scenery from outdoor tables by the resort's hidden lake, mountain, and waterfall.

High-energy lounge **Tempo (37)** *(Las Vegas Hilton, 3000 Paradise Rd., monorail stop: Las Vegas Hilton, 702-732-5111, www.lvhilton.com, 4PM–3AM)*, imbued with vestiges of the themed decor from the hotel's **Star Trek: The Experience (17)**, serves international wines and champagnes, gourmet coffees, and premium cocktails. Professional dancers and bottle-tossing bartenders add choreographed entertainment to the mix.

WHERE TO SHOP

In Las Vegas, the more appropriate question might be "Where not to shop?" Every hotel has a promenade or mall, and top retail chains pack mainstream shopping complexes such as the Fashion Show Mall (40) *(see page 76)*. Most hotel malls are open until 11PM or midnight. Tower Shops (38) *(Stratosphere Hotel, 2nd level, 2000 Las Vegas Blvd. S., closest monorail stop: Sahara, 888-236-7495 or 702-380-7777, www.stratosphere.com)* is an international marketplace of themed "streets" evoking

Paris, Hong Kong, and New York City. About 50 shops and eateries can be found here. Make shopping a journey into how the other half lives at the Esplanade (39) (*Wynn Las Vegas, 3131 Las Vegas Blvd. S., monorail stop: Las Vegas Convention Center via Wynn shuttle, 800-288-7206 or 702-733-4300, www.wynnlasvegas.com*). Where else but Las Vegas can you walk into a store for a pencil set and walk out with a Maserati? Wander through a wonderland of **Brioni**, **Cartier**, **Chanel**, **Christian Dior**, **Manolo Blahnik**, **Graff**, **John Paul Gaultier**, and more. **Wynn & Co**. is the place to go if you like the sheets you slept on or want to buy that vase in your suite bathroom. Wynn Signatures is a good spot for logo Chapstick, Wynn Mints, or a Ferrari-driving Barbie.

For items with wider appeal, take the pedestrian bridge above the traffic to the Fashion Show Mall (40) (*3200 Las Vegas Blvd. S., monorail stop: Harrah's/Imperial Palace, 702-369-0704, www.thefashionshow.com*), one of the largest enclosed malls in the world. Hub of the city's shopping scene, it boasts nearly two million square feet of climate-controlled space and 250 stores and dining outlets. Anchored by **Saks Fifth Avenue**, **Neiman Marcus**, **Bloomingdale's**, **Nordstrom**, **Dillard's**, and **Macy's**, the mall also offers an **Apple Store**, a bookstore, a chocolate café, and a kiosk selling discounted same-day show tickets amid the glass and lights. It also features the Great Hall, a multimillion-dollar event area with an 80-foot retractable runway that presents designer-line fashion shows. One of the mall's most curious features: a large multimedia "cloud" outside the Strip entrance. It's illuminated nightly and combined with four moving video screens. When not illuminated, it resembles a flying saucer parked over the mall, providing shade to diners and sidewalk amblers. One-of-a-kind shopping experiences abound in Las Vegas and many are worth a gander. Looking for fish ties, Elvis snow globes, or good old Mexican jumping beans? Look no further than mammoth souvenir emporium **Bonanza Gift Shop (41)** *(2440 Las Vegas Blvd. S. at Sahara Ave., 702-385-7359, www.worldslargestgiftshop.com)*, which tags itself as the largest gift shop in the world. **Don Pablo Cigar Company (42)** *(3049 Las Vegas Blvd. S., #25, 800-537-4957 or 702-369-1818, www.donpablo cigars.com)* specializes in traditional premium hand-rolled Cuban-style cigars. Come at the right time and watch the stogies materialize in the Master Cigar Makers' deft fingers.

WHERE TO STAY

When the **Stratosphere ($) (43)** *(2000 Las Vegas Blvd. S., closest monorail stop: Sahara, 888-236-7495 or 702-380-7777, www.stratosphere.com)* opened in 1996 on the former site of Vegas World in a seedier side of town, it had been ballyhooed as local entrepreneur Bob Stupak's boondoggle and suffered fires, accidents, even bankruptcy. But in Vegas, dreams may vanquish the odds—the property was sold, survived, and took its place as a city icon. You'll thrill to the spectacular views from its tower, though its many low-rise rooms are stacked at the base. (Note: You can request an upper-floor **Premier Tower** room with view.) Accommodations are handsome and inexpensive, and your stay includes use of the fitness center (daily fees charged). You can also take complimentary rides to the **Stratosphere Tower (1)** *(see page 61)* **Observation Deck** (a $10.95 value) before noon. Although located away from the Strip, the hotel is close to both Downtown and Sahara monorail stops.

Who can resist staying where the Beatles once holed up? The **Sahara ($) (44)** *(2535 Las Vegas Blvd. S., monorail stop: Sahara, 888-696-2121 or 702-267-9668, www. saharavegas.com)* is the only Las Vegas hotel claiming that bragging right. Although the theme is Moroccan Casbah, the interior focus is emphatically NASCAR,

thanks to a mid-1990s multimillion-dollar face-lift. The two do not necessarily mix in anything but humor, but this 1952 Vegas hotel mainstay has earned the right to be anything it wants to be. Consider the suites in its **Tangiers Tower**, which carry some of the hotel's original Middle Eastern motif.

The gleaming cocoa monolith with the 50-floor-high white script shadowing the Strip is **Wynn Las Vegas ($$$) (45)** *(3131 Las Vegas Blvd. S., monorail stop: Las Vegas Convention Center via Wynn shuttle, 800-288-7206 or 702-733-4300, www.wynnlasvegas.com)*. Centrally located and chock-full of eye candy and amenities (the Tom Fazio–designed champion golf course that is the hotel's backyard is the only golfing available on the Strip), this is the current "it" hotel (that is, until the next one opens). Its main entrance is bedecked by a sunlit display of glass flowers, a munchkin-esque floral fantasy created by master glassblower Dale Chihuly. The hotel's rooms offer wow-factor decor, quality linens, comfortable beds, and views. Rooms are large and offer floor-to-ceiling windows, a sitting area, flat-screen high-def TVs in bedroom and bath, cordless phone, fax, and high-speed Internet. A VIP desk with lounge and refreshments is available for an extra fee. The hotel connects to the Fashion Show Mall (40) *(see page 72)* via a bridge over Las Vegas Boulevard. It also provides a shuttle much of the day to the **Las Vegas Convention Center (19)** *(see page 69)* and its monorail station.

The **Las Vegas Hilton ($$) (46)** *(3000 Paradise Rd. at Riviera Blvd., monorail stop: Las Vegas Hilton, 888-732-7117 or 702-732-5111, www.lvhilton.com)* has a certain elegance, especially within its premium rooms, which offer views, high-end bedding, plasma TVs, and high-speed Internet. Or consider its newly renovated luxury suites or theme suites, done up to evoke 1920s Hollywood, the Bahamas, or an African safari. (And then there are the standard rooms.)

chapter 3

CENTRAL STRIP

CENTRAL STRIP

What to See:

1. *Sirens of TI*
2. *Mystère*
3. MIRAGE VOLCANO ★
4. Secret Garden of Siegfried and Roy
5. *LOVE*
6. Danny Gans
7. GUGGENHEIM HERMITAGE MUSEUM ★
8. Madame Tussauds
9. Wayne Brady
10. Blue Man Group
11. *Phantom of the Opera*
12. *Jersey Boys*
13. Rita Rudner
14. Auto Collections at the Imperial Palace
15. FORUM SHOPS AT CAESARS PALACE ★
16. FOUNTAINS OF BELLAGIO ★
17. BELLAGIO CONSERVATORY AND BOTANICAL GARDEN ★
18. *O*
19. *Donn Arden's Jubilee!*
20. Eiffel Tower
21. *The Producers*
22. *Stomp Out Loud*
23. *Masquerade Show in the Sky*
24. Penn & Teller
25. ATOMIC TESTING MUSEUM ★

Places to Eat & Drink:

26. Isla
27. Social House
28. Kahunaville
29. Francesco's
30. Japonais
31. Stack
32. Samba
33. Cravings
34. Bouchon
35. Valentino
36. Postrio
37. Pinot Brasserie
38. David Burke
39. Canyon Ranch Café
40. Carnevino
41. CUT
42. Table 10
43. Guy Savoy
44. Mesa Grill
45. Bradley Ogden
46. Rao's

★ *Top Picks*

*Monorail stops: Harrah's/Imperial Palace,
Flamingo/Caesars Palace, Bally's/Paris*

Hotel tram between Treasure Island and the Mirage

• SNAPSHOT •

The Central Strip became the epicenter of Las Vegas in 1989 when Steve Wynn built the Mirage, a class property on a par with those of Miami's South Beach. He put an erupting volcano in its front yard and declared the city a land of luxury and entertainment. Suddenly room rates busted three-digit ceilings, and guests began to expect more than rickety air conditioners, sandpapery bath towels, and polyester quilts steeped in years of ambient cigarette smoke.

Wynn's other innovations: an indoor rain forest, a window into a tiger's lair, swimming dolphins by the pool, swimming sharks behind  front desk clerks, and an esoteric circus troupe from Montreal. At once casinos bulged with families, "looky-loos," and scensters—new demographics interested in much more than slot machines.

These days, the sidewalks between Treasure Island ("TI") and Caesars Palace barely support the nonstop crush of tourists trying to take in the swirl of action, from the singing *Sirens of TI* and Venetian gondoliers to the singeing heat that spews from the Mirage volcano, from the nonstop Carnivale happening in front of Harrah's to the imposing Forum which heralds the wealth of today's Caesars.

WHAT TO SEE

The sultry **Sirens of TI (1)** *(Treasure Island, 3300 Las Vegas Blvd. S. at Spring Mountain Rd., monorail stop: Harrah's/Imperial Palace, 702-894-7111 or 800-944-7444, www.treasureisland.com, free, nightly at 7PM, 8:30PM, 10PM, 11:30PM)* replaced the pirates' battles that graced this hotel's "waterfront" a few years back, when the city was in its "welcome families" phase. With the subsequent abrupt shift back to "Grown-up-ville," the hotel was re-branded with the "TI" moniker,

and Victoria's Secret–style models in wet clothing stormed the pirate ships. The swashbuckling sirens sing, dance, brandish swords, and leap through crackling pyrotechnics in a 12-minute story involving the capture of a way-ward sailor and the arrival of mates who come to his rescue. The classic Cirque du Soleil production **Mystère (2)** *(Treasure Island, 3300 Las Vegas Blvd. S. at Spring Mountain Rd., monorail stop: Harrah's/Imperial Palace, 702-894-7111 or 800-944-7444, www.treasureisland.com, Sa–W 7PM and 9:30PM, Su matinee 4:30PM, dark Th)* is the troupe's first perma-nent show designed exclusively for Steve Wynn.

Though the oldest Cirque show on the strip, it retains all of its hypnotic effect and novel appeal. $60–$95. Package the show with dinner at a TI restaurant for prices that start at $126 per person *(call 866-286-3809)*.

On your way in or out of the **Mirage (81)** next door, take in its famous ★**MIRAGE VOLCANO (3)** *(Mirage, 3400 Las Vegas Blvd. S., monorail stop: Harrah's/Imperial Palace, 800-374-9000 or 702-792-7889, www.mirage.com/attractions; erupts daily on the hour: spring 7PM–midnight, summer 8PM–midnight, winter 6PM–midnight)*. Recorded sounds of birds and crickets mark the "before" and "after" of the crowd-pleasing conflagrations. The ground shakes, the 54-foot mountain thunders, and flames, smoke, and fire shoot 100 feet into the air, transforming a waterfall and three acres of water into a molten "lava" spectacle. Those standing close by will feel the heat. The show is free to the public, but may be canceled during inclement weather. When this early Steve Wynn marvel first erupted, the whole world seemed to take notice. Crowds flocked. Traffic stopped. And the volcano became a symbol of the city itself—its thrills, extravagance, and color. From that moment, the rush to come up with the next wow-factor attraction kicked into gear. Inside, in the **Secret Garden of Siegfried and Roy (4)** *(Mirage, 3400 Las Vegas Blvd. S., monorail stop: Harrah's/Imperial Palace, 800-374-9000 or 702-792-7889, www.mirage.com/attractions)*, you'll find

TOP PICK!

 white tigers, black panthers, golden tigers, snow leopards, African lions, and other fauna amid the flora. Its companion **Dolphin Habitat** is a 2.5-million-gallon pool that is the home to a family of Atlantic bottleneck dolphins. A 22-foot-deep viewing room allows you to observe them in action. Both attractions are bundled into one *(open daily: summers 10AM–7PM, rest of year 10AM or 11AM–5:30PM, call 702-791-7188)*. Admission is $15. **Tip:** A big cat lair just off the hotel lobby allows a thrilling, free glimpse at a sleeping white tiger or two most anytime day or night. *LOVE* **(5)** *(Mirage, 3400 Las Vegas Blvd. S., monorail stop: Harrah's/Imperial Palace, 800-963-9634, www.mirage.com, www.thebeatleslove.com, Th–M 7PM and 10PM)* is a new Cirque production focused on the Beatles. It uses Abbey Road Studios master tapes to create a multisensory experience involving backdrop projections of the Fab Four against a dazzling continuum of choreography, mesmerizing special effects, riveting costumes, inventive stage design, and music that reverberates through 6,341 speakers, including those built into each seat. The theater in the round projects a history of the Beatles via documentary film footage—images encircle the audience, and one behemoth video wall plays off another. As the music intensifies, old London appears to rise in an atmospheric panorama of rooftops, the Beatles recess into shadows, the music riffs into various numbers, and clownlike

characters move in intriguing interpretations of the hit songs. Tickets range from $69 to $150. The magic continues with **Danny Gans (6)** *(Mirage, 3400 Las Vegas Blvd. S., monorail stop: Harrah's/Imperial Palace, 702-792-7777 or 800-963-9634, www.mirage.com, Tu–W, F–Sa 8PM; dark M, Th, Su)*, a master of impressions who morphs from Ricky

Martin, to Smokey Robinson, to Joe Cocker, to James Brown, to Blood, Sweat, and Tears in the time it takes to wipe your glasses. He keeps some 300 celebrity personalities in his pocket, and the audience never knows whom he's going to pull out. The Seinfeld look-alike also belts out tunes in voices ranging from Billy Joel, David Bowie, and Bruce Springsteen to Anita Baker, Natalie Cole, and Macy Gray. Tickets run $100.

Across the street, inside the **Venetian (82)**, view some of the world's greatest art at the ★**GUGGENHEIM HERMITAGE MUSEUM (7)** *(Venetian, 3355 Las Vegas Blvd. S., monorail stop: Harrah's/Imperial Palace, 702-414-2440, www.guggenheimlasvegas.org, daily 9:30AM–7:30PM).* A partnership between the Guggenheim Foundation and the State Hermitage Museum in St. Petersburg, Russia, and periodic collaborations with the Kunsthistorisches Museum in Vienna, the museum provides visitors with an opportunity to view

TOP PICK!

a range of paintings, sculptures, furnishings, jewelry, and more, including pieces not often seen in the U.S. Rooms designed by famed architect **Rem Koolhaas** showcase revolving collections in a streamlined space that features earth-toned Cor-Ten "weathering steel" construction. The textured metal succeeds in its mission to evoke the velvet walls of the Winter Palace of Catherine the Great, while providing an almost icy modern contrast to the hotel's sumptuous architecture. General admission is $15. From artwork to waxworks: **Madame Tussauds (8)** *(Venetian, 3355 Las Vegas Blvd. S., monorail stop: Harrah's/Imperial Palace, 702-862-7800, www. mtvegas.com, 10AM–10:30PM, general admission: $24)* may be as close as you'll ever get to Brad Pitt, Johnny Depp, or Jennifer Lopez. You can play instruments with the Blue Man Group and even "marry" George Clooney without his consent (ideal if you have intimacy problems and would rather wed a wax statue). Accessible from the sidewalk, the attraction is a fun way to beat the heat with Britney or rest your feet with Barbra. **Wayne Brady (9)** *(Venetian, 3355 Las Vegas Blvd. S. at Sands Ave., monorail stop: Harrah's/Imperial Palace, 702-414-9000 or 877-883-6423, www.venetian.com, Th–M 9PM)* and his "Making It Up" show spotlight the hilarious improvisational skills of the performer best known for his antics on the "Whose Line Is It Anyway?" **Tip:** VIP tickets include front-row seating and an after-show meet-and-greet with the star. Tickets start at $49. Percussion and pranks await during an evening with **Blue Man Group (10)** *(Venetian, 3355 Las Vegas Blvd. S. at Sands Ave., monorail stop: Harrah's/Imperial Palace,*

702-414-9000 or 877-883-6423, www.venetian.com, shows daily, times vary). They play plumbing pipes, they paint, they feed odd foods to audience members, they pantomime, they pour iridescent colors into their mouths, but they never speak. The show is mesmerizing, and the music pumps. Tickets run $76.50 to $128.50. The **Phantom of the Opera** (11) *(Venetian, 3355 Las Vegas*

Blvd. S. at Sands Ave., monorail stop: Harrah's/Imperial Palace, 702-414-9000 or 877-883-6423, www.phantom lasvegas.com, shows daily except Su, times vary) haunts Las Vegas with a new, 90-minute production, complete with special effects created exclusively for this stage. Tickets $75 to $150. Note: For $250 per person, you can enjoy a **VIP experience** that includes a backstage tour, private meet-and-greet with the cast, and special seating.

Another export from Broadway, **Jersey Boys** (12) *(Palazzo, 3525 Las Vegas Blvd. S., monorail stop: Harrah's/Imperial Palace, 866-263-3001, www.palazzo lasvegas.com),* the 2006 Best Musical Tony-Award winner, anoints the new theater in the **Palazzo** (83) and recounts the story of Frankie Valli and the Four Seasons.

A few doors down, **Rita Rudner** (13) *(Harrah's, 3475 Las Vegas Blvd. S., monorail stop: Harrah's/Imperial Palace, 702-407-6000, 702-369-5222 or 800-214-9110, www.harrahs.com, M–Sa 8PM, dark Su),* first lady of ironic comedy, skewers men, relationships, shopping, and other topics. $54.

Car buffs can check out Marilyn Monroe's 1955 coral-pink Lincoln Capri Convertible or "Eleanor," the 1967 Ford Mustang used in the movie *Gone in Sixty Seconds*, at the **Auto Collections at the Imperial Palace (14)** *(Imperial Palace, parking garage 5th floor, 3535 Las Vegas Blvd. S., monorail stop: Harrah's/Imperial Palace, 800-634-6441 or 702-794-3174, www.autocollections.com, daily 9:30AM–9:30PM)*. The 125,000-square-foot showroom displays a rotating collection of 250 vehicles, including the world's largest collection of Duesenbergs—25 of them, built between 1925 and 1937. You'll also find such beauties as a 1966 Ferrari 500, a 1994 Jaguar XJ220, or a 1987 Camaro convertible for sale. Admission is $6.95. **Tip:** Check Web site *(www.auto collections.com)* for free admission passes before you go.

TOP PICK!

Even if you hate to shop, you'll still be impressed by the ★**FORUM SHOPS AT CAESARS PALACE (15)** *(Caesars Palace, 3570 Las Vegas Blvd. S., monorail stop: Flamingo/Caesars Palace, 702-731-7110 or 866-227-5938, www.harrahs. com)*. It opened in 1992 as an ancient Roman metropolis, complete with a "sky" of changing hues over an opulent cityscape with

lighted windows, balconies, fountains, and animated statuary. It's pure entertainment every evening! Take a circular escalator between tiers or sit and watch the crowds go by with a latte, cognac, or handcrafted Arturo Fuente cigar at **Casa Fuente** tobacco shop and bistro *(702-731-5051)*, one of the few non-casino indoor places in Vegas where you can still smoke. Keep your eyes open for familiar faces. Experience 24 hours in 60 minutes as the faux firmament turns from dawn to dusk, enjoy the 50,000-gallon saltwater aquarium, or watch stuffed animals work and play in the FAO Schwarz window display. And don't miss the free animated fountain shows. At the **Festival Fountain** *(west end of the mall just beyond the Planet Hollywood restaurant, every hour on the hour)*, Venus, Apollo, Pluto, and Bacchus raise and lower their hands and jiggle their heads in a seven-minute sound-and-laser light show. The volume turns up on the **Fall of Atlantis Fountain** *(by the aquarium in front of the Cheesecake Factory café, on the hour from 10AM–midnight)*, an animatronic battle-to-the-death for the mythic land beneath the sea, waged between the gods of fire, water, and ice. This show, too, lasts about seven minutes.

Resort mogul Steve Wynn's famous ★FOUNTAINS OF BELLAGIO (16) *(Bellagio, 3600 Las Vegas Blvd. S. at Flamingo Rd., monorail stop: Bally's/Paris, 702-693-7111 or 888-987-6667, www.bellagio.com)* is a Vegas must-see.

TOP PICK!

The fountains' 11-acre "Lake Como" reflects the Strip's neon in its normally calm waters and pastel-hued sprays. But every half-hour *(from 3PM–midnight)*, it erupts in music and dance. Jets of water soar as high as 240 feet as songs such as "Fly Me to the Moon" sail out of the speakers. More than 1,000 "water expressions" and 4,000 lights spring into action. Observers will notice three types of effects: "oarsmen," which cause the fountains to swing back and forth in dancing moves; "shooters," which shoot water upward; and "super shooters," blasting columns of water into the sky. The $40 million show is free. Catch it from the patio on the lake at **Fontana Bar**, or for maximum romance, watch from under the twinkle lights at a bistro-style table, al fresco, across the street at **Mon Ami Gabi, Paris Las Vegas (89)**. One of the most amazing gardens west of Versailles has

TOP PICK!

to be the ★**BELLAGIO CONSERVATORY AND BOTANICAL GARDEN (17)** *(Bellagio, off the lobby, 3600 Las Vegas Blvd. S., at Flamingo Rd., monorail stop: Bally's/Paris, 702-693-7111 or 888-987-6667, www.bellagio.com; new displays are unveiled each year on Jan. 12 for Chinese New Year, March 15, May 17, Sept. 13, and Dec. 1).* A staff of over 100 people transforms this three-story, 13,573-square-foot space into astounding fairy-tale gardens five times a year. Twenty-five-foot redwoods, 40-foot poplars, azaleas, hydrangeas, and dahlias, to name just a few, are shipped in from all over and arranged on a puzzlelike platform system. The heady fragrances of 10,000 plantings are enhanced by lights, sounds, gazebos, bridges, and water features. A recent "Route 66"–themed display included a classic Corvette, hot air balloons, even a 42-foot Ferris wheel amid myriad rosebushes and rows of sunflowers. The stage of **Cirque du Soleil**'s beautiful *O* **(18)** *(Bellagio, 3600 Las Vegas Blvd. S., monorail stop: Bally's/Paris Las Vegas, 702-693-7722 or 888-488-7111, www.bellagio.com, W–Su 7:30PM and 10:30PM)* broke the C-note threshold for Vegas shows and created a new trend in high-end entertainment. The stage is a 25-foot-deep pool filled with 1.5 million gallons of water; the show that transpires is a hypnotic whirlwind of color, costume, and splash set to music. Tickets run $99 to $150.

In the mid-1970s, **Bally's (86)** was the original, ultra-glamorous MGM Grand. This is where you'll find the second-longest-running follies-style revue in Vegas: *Donn Arden's Jubilee!* **(19)** *(Bally's, 3645 Las Vegas Blvd. S., monorail stop: Bally's/Paris, 702-739-4111, 877-603-4390 or 800-237-SHOW, www.harrahs.com, Sa–Th 7:30PM and 10:30PM)*. This must-see production is famous for its million-dollar sets, lavish Bob Mackie costumes, and leggy beauties (voted the town's "Best Showgirls"), performing classic routines that climax in an eye-catching finale that recreates the sinking of the *Titanic*. Seats start at $48. Add a **Showgirl Meet-and-Greet**

($50 extra for one person, $35 each for two or more). The experience includes a complimentary cocktail, a conversation with a tall young woman in feathers and fishnets, a photo of the two of you, a signed souvenir program, and VIP admission.

Très magnifique! Rendezvous atop the **Eiffel Tower (20)** *(Paris Las Vegas, 3655 Las Vegas Blvd. S., monorail stop: Bally's/Paris, 702-946-7000, www.paris lasvegas.com, 9:30AM–12:30AM)*. A convincing replica of the Paris original at half the scale, the steel structure rises 460 feet above the Strip. The **"Eiffel Tower Experience"** elevator *($9, tickets available at box office and Eiffel Tour gift shop)* will whisk you from the casino to the 50th floor in 90 seconds. Its operator offers factoids about both towers, and you can enjoy the observation platform as long as you wish. **Tip:** The elevator holds only eight to ten people; expect lines at peak times. *The Producers* **(21)** *(Paris Las Vegas, 3655 Las Vegas Blvd. S., monorail stop: Bally's/Paris, reservations 888-727-4758, www.parislasvegas.com, M–F 8PM, Sa 6PM and 9PM)* brings the Broadway hit to the Strip with a revolving cast of talent that has included Tony Danza and David Hasselhoff. Tickets $69 to $143.

Stomp Out Loud **(22)** *(Planet Hollywood, 3667 Las Vegas Blvd. S., monorail stop: Bally's/Paris, 702-785-5000 or 877-333-9474, www.planethollywoodresort.com or www. stomponline.com, Su–F 8PM, Sa 7PM)*, from the folks who brought you the original *Stomp*, presents a lively performance of percussion, movement, and visual comedy. Tickets range from $50 to $110.

A few blocks west, you'll come across a **Brazilian Carnivale** of sorts: the *Masquerade Show in the Sky* **(23)** *(Rio, 3700 W. Flamingo Rd. at Valley View Blvd., monorail stop: Harrah's/Imperial Palace, 702-252-7777, www.harrahs.com, daily every hour or so from 3PM to midnight)*. Exotic-looking, masked performers in brilliant costumes celebrate atop strangely beautiful yet grotesque floats suspended from the ceiling. Yes, you may buy tickets ($12.95 each) and ride along with the performers during the 20-minute show. Those "Bad Boys of Magic" **Penn & Teller (24)** *(Rio, 3700 W. Flamingo Rd., at Hotel Rio Dr., monorail stop: not accessible, 702-777-7776 or 866-746-7671, www.playrio.com, Sa–Th 9PM)* combine magic and comedy in outrageous live performances that might include guns, knives, a fire-eating showgirl, or a duck. Seats start at $75.

Las Vegas has museums, lots of them, nearly all one of a kind. For example, where else can you experience a "you-are-there" atomic blast red alert re-creation in a concrete bunker? At the ★**ATOMIC TESTING MUSEUM (25)** *(755 E. Flamingo Rd. at Swenson, 702-794-5161, www.atomic testingmuseum.org, M–Sa 9AM–5PM, Su 1PM–5PM)*, where else? The museum

TOP PICK!

takes you through more than 50 years of testing with exhibits and demonstrations that offer a powerful look at atomic milestones of the 20th and 21st centuries. You'll find a respected library here, as well as retired

Nevada Test Site engineers who are available for stories and questions. A cool gift shop offers unique, if not off-color, mementos. Admission for adults is $12.

PLACES TO EAT & DRINK
Where to Eat:

Visit award-winning ("Best Mexican Restaurant," *Las Vegas Life* magazine) **Isla (26)** *(Treasure Island, 3000 Las Vegas Blvd. S., 702-894-7111, www.treasureisland.com, Su–Th 4PM–11PM, W, F, Sa 4PM–midnight)* to sample chef Richard Sandoval's modern twist on the cuisine.

The bar's "Tequila Goddess" welcomes patrons with enticing cocktails. The one to watch at Treasure Island (80) ("TI") is **Social House (27) ($$$)** *(Treasure Island, 3300 Las Vegas Blvd. S., monorail stop: Harrah's/Imperial Palace, 702-894-7111, www.treasureisland.com, open M–W until midnight, Th–Su until 2AM)*, truly "eater-tainment." This **Nobu Matsuhisa**-created sushi/sake joint for scenesters features a live DJ and interactive sushi bar. Its outdoor patio lounge offers seats on the Strip and provides VIP viewing of the sexy *Sirens of TI* (1) *(see page 84)* in front of the hotel. Indoor dining provides several intimate, semi-private dining areas. In the mood for Kobe beef or Tasmanian freshwater fish? You'll find it here. **Kahunaville (28) ($)** *(Treasure Island, 3300 Las Vegas Blvd. S., monorail stop: Harrah's/Imperial Palace, 702-894-7390, www.kahunaville.com, 8AM–10PM, open until 3AM weekends)* is all about fried, Mexican, and Cajun comfort food with color. It touts itself as a tropical hot spot, offering island-infused drinks mixed by bottle-flipping bartenders and delivered by gyrating servers. The beach-party ambience is enhanced by a dancing water show and

dueling pianists. At **Francesco's (29) ($$)** *(Treasure Island, 3300 Las Vegas Blvd. S., monorail stop: Harrah's/ Imperial Palace, 702-894-7223, Sa–W 5PM–10:30PM, www.treasureisland.com)*, expect traditional lasagna and chicken parmigiana dripping in hearty red sauce. The wall art is what makes this family-style, semi-gourmet room different. Between the Mediterranean sconces and Tuscan touches hang works of art by such entertainment icons as Tony Bennett, Tony Curtis, and Phyllis Diller.

Next door, **Japonais (30) ($$$)** *(Mirage, 3400 Las Vegas Blvd. S., monorail stop: Harrah's/Imperial Palace, 866-339-4566, www.japonaislasvegas.com, 5PM–11PM daily)* is a new kid on the block (and a rich kid at that). Like its Chicago and New York incarnations, it offers con-

temporary Japanese fusion cuisine and unusual sushi creations. Located just inside the casino, the restaurant evokes a garden one might find in a hip section of Kyoto. The must-have dish: "The Rock," thin-sliced mari-nated New York strip steak cooked on a hot rock tableside. For s'mores martinis, miso-soaked cod in lettuce cups, free-range organic chicken, and 24-ounce cowboy steaks, make it the

Stack (31) ($$-$$$) *(Mirage, 3400 Las Vegas Blvd. S., monorail stop: Harrah's/Imperial Palace, 866-339-4566, www.mirage.com, Su–Th, 5PM–11PM, F–Sa 5PM–midnight)*, where walls are layered in warm woods. Expect loud music, crowded surrounds, and scrumptious food. Cap off the experience with a round of jelly doughnut holes. Carnivores savor **Samba (32) ($$)** *(Mirage, 3400 Las Vegas Blvd. S., monorail stop: Harrah's/Imperial Palace, 702-791-7111, www.mirage.com, daily*

5PM–10:30PM), a Brazilian-style steakhouse where menu choices, roasted on skewers, arrive non-stop at your table until you beg the waitstaff to cease and desist. Try the beef empanadas with homemade hot sauce or Amazon-style spicy chicken wings dusted with peanuts and cashews. Buffet **Cravings (33) ($)** *(Mirage, 3400 Las Vegas Blvd. S., monorail stop: Harrah's/Imperial Palace, 702-791-7777, www.mirage.com, 7AM–10PM)* offers an open, expansive Adam Tihany–designed dining room full of visual movement, with 11 cooking stations offering Korean delights as well as Japanese, Chinese, Italian, and mainstream fare. (Note: In a nod to tradition, former owner Steve Wynn's mother's bread pudding is still served as well.)

The **Venetian (82)** boasts its share of celeb-chef power with such restaurants as **Bouchon (34) ($$-$$$)** (*Venetian, 3355 Las Vegas Blvd. S., monorail stop: Harrah's/Imperial Palace, 702-414-6200, www.venetian.com, daily 7AM–10:30AM, 5PM–11PM, Sa–Su 11:30AM–2:30PM*), from **Thomas Keller**, of Napa Valley's French Laundry. Entrées include steak frites and *boudin noir* (blood sausage with sautéed apples). **Tip:** Breakfasts are a treat here, for views, setting, home-baked brioche, and fab French toast served bread-pudding style. **Piero Selvaggio's Valentino (35) ($$$)** (*Venetian, 3355 Las Vegas Blvd. S., monorail stop: Harrah's/Imperial Palace, 702-414-3000, www.venetian.com, daily 11:30AM–11PM*) complements its fine Italian cuisine with a 24,000-bottle wine list. **Wolfgang Puck's Postrio (36) ($-$$$)** (*Venetian, 3355 Las Vegas Blvd. S., monorail stop: Harrah's/Imperial Palace, 702-796-1110, www.wolfgangpuck.com*) presents two dining experiences—the café (*Su–Th 11:30AM–10PM, F–Sa until 11PM*) serving Puck's signature wood-oven pizzas and lobster clubs, and a more formal dining room (*Su–Th 5:30PM–10PM, F–Sa until 11PM*). **Joachim Splichal's** casual California-French bistro **Pinot Brasserie (37) ($-$$$)** (*Venetian, 3355 Las Vegas Blvd. S., monorail stop: Harrah's/Imperial Palace, 702-414-8888, www.venetian.com, breakfast M–F 8AM–10AM, Sa–Su 8AM–3PM, lunch daily 11:30AM–3PM, dinner Su–Th 5:30PM–10PM, F–Sa 5:30PM–10:30PM*) offers seafood, steaks, and an unforgettable chocolate soufflé. **David Burke (38) ($$$)**

(Venetian, 3355 Las Vegas Blvd. S. at Sands Ave., mono-rail stop: Harrah's/Imperial Palace, 702-414-7111, www.davidburkelasvegas.net, Su–Th 5PM–10PM, F–Sa 5PM–11PM) combines humor with ultra-sleek design. Expect such items as a "crisp and angry" lobster cocktail, a cheesecake lollipop tree, and pretzel-crusted crab cakes. For lean and healthy cuisine, make it **Canyon Ranch Café (39) ($)** *(Venetian, Canyon Ranch Spa, 3355 Las Vegas Blvd. S., monorail stop: Harrah's/Imperial Palace, 702-414-3633, www.venetian.com, 7AM–6PM)*, serving exquisite spa food. Dine in or take out to the private pool area.

Palazzo (83), right next to the **Venetian (82)**, boasts 14 new restaurants from renowned chefs. **Carnevino (40) ($$$)** *(Palazzo, 3325 Las Vegas Blvd. S., monorail stop: Harrah's/Imperial Palace, 702-414-4300, www.palazzo lasvegas.com)* opened by chef Mario Batali and wine-maker Joe Bastianich merge their individual talents, featuring high-quality American meat paired with an international wine list. **Wolfgang Puck**'s, **CUT (41) ($$$)** *(Palazzo, 3325 Las Vegas Blvd. S., monorail stop: Harrah's/Imperial Palace, 702-607-6300, www.palazzo lasvegas.com)*, a contemporary twist on a classic steak-house, is his sixth restaurant to open in Vegas. Adjacent to the restaurant is a bar and lounge with specialty cock-tails and a smaller menu, featuring Mini Kobe Beef Sliders, its signature appetizer. Cajun **Table 10 (42) ($$–$$$)** *(Palazzo, 3325 Las Vegas Blvd. S., monorail stop: Harrah's/Imperial Palace, 702-414-4300, www.palazzo lasvegas.com)* is **Emeril Lagasse**'s third location in Las

Vegas. The name comes from the chef's original Crescent City restaurant; Table 10 is where he discussed ideas and planned menus with his staff.

Caesars Palace (85) has a firmly-planted footprint in the Vegas dining scene, most recently with the addition of **Guy Savoy (43) ($$$)** *(Caesars Palace, 3570 Las Vegas Blvd. S., monorail stop: Flamingo/Caesars Palace, 877-346-4642, www.caesarspalace.com, W–Su 5:30PM–10:30PM)*, the Michelin-starred chef's only U.S. venue. Adjacent to the dining room: **Bubble Bar**, featuring a sampling from Savoy's kitchen. A real bargain—four plates for $40. You'll also find a restaurant created by Bobby Flay—the **Mesa Grill (44) ($$$)** *(Caesars Palace, 3570 Las Vegas Blvd. S.,*

monorail stop: Flamingo/Caesars Palace, 702-731-7731, www.caesarspalace.com, daily 11AM–2:30PM, 5PM–11PM), serving Southwestern fare, and **Bradley Ogden (45) ($$$)** *(Caesars Palace, 3570 Las Vegas Blvd. S., monorail stop: Flamingo/Caesars Palace, 877-346-4642, www.caesarspalace.com, daily 5PM–11PM)*, offering classic American. A fun spot to spend lunch or dinner: **Rao's (46) ($$$)** *(Caesars Palace, 3570 Las Vegas Blvd. S., monorail stop: Flamingo/Caesars Palace, 877-346-4642, www.caesarspalace.com, daily 6AM–11AM, 5PM–11PM)*, another newcomer. Its original Harlem location is called "the finest place you will never dine" because of its 11-only tables, either pre-booked years in advance or pre-owned by influential "families." The behemoth Vegas version gives regular guys and gals a shot at the *pasta e fagioli* and shrimp scampi.

Bellagio (88) is a veritable mall of master chef dining outlets. **Le Cirque (47) ($$$)** *(Bellagio, 3600 Las Vegas Blvd. S., monorail stop: Bally's/Paris, 877-2-DINE-LV or 877-234-6358, www.bellagio.com, daily 5:30PM–10PM)*, a re-creation of **Sirio Maccioni**'s gustatory temple in New York, is set in animated surrounds and presents colorfully rustic yet elegant French cookery. **Prime Steakhouse (48) ($$$)** *(Bellagio, 3600 Las Vegas Blvd. S., monorail stop: Bally's/Paris, 877-234-6358, www.bellagio.com, daily 5PM–10PM)*, the playground of chef **Jean-Georges Vongerichten**, puts food and fountain views lakeside. Expect Baccarat chandeliers, plush furnishings, and gilding galore in this 1930s-style speakeasy. Après-meal, the outdoor patio is a lovely spot for handcrafted cocktails and cigars. The soaring cove ceilings, intimate nooks, and fine art of **Picasso (49) ($$$)** *(Bellagio, 3600 Las Vegas Blvd. S., monorail stop: Bally's/Paris, 877-234-6358, www.bellagio.com, W–M 6PM–9:30PM)* make it a sensational setting for French-Mediterranean cuisine (even if Julia Roberts is not dining at the next table). **Julian Serrano**, James Beard winner of "Best Chef, Southwest," showcases seasonal cuisine in a four-course tasting menu and five-course Chef's Degustation. **Michael Mina (50) ($$$)** *(Bellagio, 3600 Las Vegas Blvd. S., monorail stop: Bally's/Paris, 877-234-6358, www.bellagio.com, daily 5:30PM–10PM)* presents this culinary artist's innovative seafood menu;

California and Mediterranean ingredients are complemented by distinguished wines from around the world.

Eiffel Tower Restaurant (51) ($$$) *(Paris, 3655 Las Vegas Blvd. S., monorail stop: Bally's/Paris, 702-948-6937, www.eiffeltowerrestaurant.com, lunch daily 11AM–3:30PM dinner Su–Th 5PM-10PM, F–Sa 5PM–10:30PM).* Take in stunning views 11 stories above the epicenter of the Strip. Accurately replicated girders of Gustave Eiffel's famed French tower offer an authentic sense of place (if you ignore the neon, that is). Relax with a cocktail, such as "La Vie en Rose"—pearl of pomegranate vodka and rose nectar. Try tournedos of beef or a truffle sauce–type entrée. Cap off your meal with a dessert soufflé. **Le Village Buffet (52) ($)** *(Paris, 3655 Las Vegas Blvd. S., monorail stop: Bally's/Paris, 702-946-7000, www.paris lasvegas.com, breakfast daily 7AM–11AM, lunch M–F 11AM–3:30PM, dinner M–Th, Su 3:30PM–10PM, F–Sa 3:30PM–11PM, champagne brunch Sa–Su 11AM–3:30PM)*

ranks among the city's better places to enjoy a smorgasbord. The menu includes haute recipes and French sauces and the layout is warm and welcoming, with Gallic country appeal and a variety of spaces in which to dine, from "outside" on the town square to "inside" by the fire. Next door, **Spice Market Buffet (53) ($)** *(Planet Hollywood, 3667 Las Vegas Blvd. S., monorail* *stop: Bally's/Paris, 702-785-9005 or 866-919-7472, www.planethollywoodresort.com)* is probably among the city's best buffets for the price (dinner is $24.99). Stations include Middle Eastern and Indian favorites, from shish kebab to tandoori chicken, as well as Mongolian barbecue, Chinese stir fry, hot and cold seafood, sushi and sashimi, and a showcase of home-made desserts. Dig into the only all-seafood cornucopia in town at **Village Seafood Buffet (54) ($$)** *(Rio, 3700 W. Flamingo Rd. at Hotel Rio Dr., monorail stop: not accessible, 702-777-7777, www.playrio.com, Su–Th 4PM–10PM, F–Sa 4PM–11PM)*. Go for bouillabaisse by the bowl-after-bowlful, plus lobster tail, snow crab legs, oysters, and sushi with no limits on seconds. There's prime rib for meat eaters, pastas aplenty, and fresh-baked bread.

The **Hard Rock Hotel & Casino (91)** has star chefs of its

own. **Kerry Simon**, a cuisinier with rock star looks, opened **Simon (55) ($$$)** *(Hard Rock, 4455 Paradise Rd. at Harmon, monorail stop: not accessible, 702-693-4440, www.hardrockhotel.com, M–Th 5:30PM–10:30PM, Sa–Su 5:30PM–11:30PM)* serves American-fusion com-fort creations—wasabi mashed potatoes, tandoori salmon, Simon meatloaf, caramel apple crisp, cotton candy dessert—to a constel-lation-driven clientele (think Jagger, McCartney, Bowie, Willis, Clooney). **Nobu (56) ($$$)** *(Hard Rock, 4455 Paradise Rd. at Harmon, monorail stop: not accessible,*

702-693-5090, www.hardrockhotel.com, daily 6PM–11PM) brings the tastes and talents of sushi master and stylist **Nobu Matsuhisa** to Las Vegas. This is one of the few places to get fresh Kumamoto oysters or genuine Washu beef. Experience a true Omakase evening here with a multicourse, prix-fixe chef's choice menu, something rarely offered stateside. As you might expect, sushi and sashimi cuts here are legendary.

Nearby **Alizé (57) ($$$)** *(Palms, 4321 W. Flamingo Rd. at Arville St., monorail stop: not accessible, 702-951-7000, www.andrelv.com, 5:30PM–close)* is chef **André Rochat**'s stamp on (or just off) the Strip with savory fondues, Pernod-laced scampi, and dramatic views more than 50 stories above. **Nove (58) ($$$)** *(Palms, 4321 W. Flamingo Rd. at Arville St., monorail stop: not accessible, 702-942-6800, www.palms.com, daily 5PM–11PM)* recently opened in the **Palms Fantasy Tower** *(see page 118)* and combines stunning views with dishes prepared "the Italian way," whether on the grill, tossed with pasta, or enhanced with extra virgin olive oil or a squeeze of lemon. Its high-style interiors, resembling those found in mansions around La La Land, attract a youthful, monied Hollywood. It's no wonder the **Playboy Club** *(see page 110)* opened next door.

Bars & Nightlife:

It's all happening at the resorts. **Tangerine (59)** *(Treasure Island, 3300 Las Vegas Blvd. S., monorail stop: Harrah's/Imperial Palace, 702-894-7580, www.treasure island.com, Th–Su 9PM–4AM)* is a sweet spot, full of late-night action in a hodgy-podgy speakeasy setting, complete with burlesque queens and orange modular furniture. The outdoor lounge looking over **Sirens' Cove** (formerly Buccaneer Bay) makes it stranger (yet sweeter). A DJ spins, and crowds dance. Periodic interruptions by live saxophone, percussion, and stand-up bass back steamy burlesque performances.

The **Mirage (81)** next door *(connected to Treasure Island by private tram)* recently opened **Revolution Lounge (60)** *(Mirage, 3400 Las Vegas Blvd. S., monorail stop: Harrah's/Imperial Palace, 702-692-8383, www.thebeatles revolutionlounge.com, daily 6PM–4AM)*. An homage to Cirque du Soleil's *LOVE (5) (see page 86)*, it bills itself as an interactive Beatles lounge and is currently among the hottest on the Strip. **JET Nightclub (61)** *(Mirage, 3400 Las Vegas Blvd. S., monorail stop: Harrah's/Imperial Palace, 702-693-8300, www.jet vegas.com, F–Sa, M 10:30PM–4AM)* features a light-and-laser grid with state-of-the-art audio and cryogenic effects in three distinct rooms, each with its own dance floor, DJ booth, and sound system.

Across the street, **Tao (62)** *(Venetian, 3355 Las Vegas Blvd. S., monorail stop: Harrah's/Imperial Palace, 702-388-8588, www.taolasvegas.com, 5PM–close)* is getting a good deal of buzz these days as one of the hottest clubs in town, with probably the priciest cabana scene night or day. The 40,000 square foot, $20-million design-driven dining/entertainment complex attracts the glitterati with three-tiered "Asian city" appeal and techno-Zen decor. Its outside terrace offers Strip views, a hot pool scene, private skyboxes with mini-bars, and cabanas rentable for the evening at four-figure sums.

Jay-Z's trendy **40/40 Club (63)** *(Palazzo, 3325 Las Vegas Blvd. S., monorail stop: Harrah's/Imperial Palace, 866-263-3001, www.palazzo lasvegas.com)* combines sports memorabilia with a lavish interior. The Latin-soul menu tempts with Southern-fried chicken sticks and more.

At Caesars Palace (85), the "Can-you-top-this?" nightclubs include **Pure (64)** *(Caesars, 3570 Las Vegas Blvd. S., monorail stop: Flamingo/Caesars Palace, 702-731-PURE [7873], www.purethenightclub.com, F–Su 10PM–early AM)*, with three venues: a dance floor surrounded by draped bed spaces in the **Main Room**, a private VIP **Red Room** for those of a certain refinement, and a glass elevator to the **Terrace**, a hidden enclave on the hotel deck with private spaces and panoramic views of the neon. The attached **Pussycat Dolls (65)** *(Caesars, 3570 Las Vegas Blvd. S., monorail stop: Flamingo/Caesars Palace, 702-369-5000, www.pcdlounge.com, shows begin 10:30PM)*

space brings the group's seductive arts to town in acts in which the Dolls, clad in fishnets, leather, and bustiers, pop out of champagne glasses, drop from the ceiling on swings, and sing, dance, and entertain audiences from the floor and stage.

Bellagio (88) offers two spots worth the stop for scene-seeking visitors. **Bank (66)** *(Bellagio, 3600 Las Vegas Blvd. S., monorail stop: Bally's/Paris, 702-693-8300, www.light group.com, Th–Su 10PM–4AM)* is the nightclub with the bouncer and the velvet rope; once you're in, you'll find a large, dark room with glam servers in tight, high-slit black velvet gowns and an elite crowd. Tables are for European bottle service only, and they do fill up. Located inside the casino, **Caramel (67)** *(Bellagio, 3600 Las Vegas Blvd. S., monorail stop: Bally's/Paris, 702-693-8300, www.caramelbar.com, M–Tu 5PM–3AM, W–Su 5PM–4AM)* is a bit more casual. No bouncers, no cover, no questions. Just intimate tables, atmosphere, and high-priced martinis in a multitude of flavors.

The **Hard Rock Hotel & Casino (91)** might be the first place you'd look for the scene, and you would be right. The pool is "party central" night and day throughout the summer, with hired babes who make sure the action never stops. **The Joint** at the hotel presents top name musical talent in a smaller space. The **Body English (68)** *(Hard Rock Hotel & Casino, 4455 Paradise Rd., 702-693-5000, www.bodyenglish.com, W–Su 10:30PM–4AM)* nightclub exudes European appeal with Baccarat crystal chandeliers, rich leather booths, and black walls. Lots of VIP-only spaces here, but there is ample room for commoners as well.

Voodoo Lounge (69) *(Rio, 51st floor, 3700 W. Flamingo Rd. at Hotel Rio Dr., monorail stop: not accessible, 702-492-3960, www.voodoolv.com, daily 8PM–3AM)* has the views, the music, the atmosphere, and the big red drinks. The interior is a scary black-lit Cajun affair with libations to match; the club opens onto an open-air balcony above town. Getting into the elevator without waiting in line will cost you, unless you dine at the restaurant a floor below. The latest club of sorts to hit the city: **Lucky Strike Lanes (70)** *(Rio, 702-777-7999, www.luckystrikelv.com, daily 11AM–3AM, 21-and-over only after 9PM)*. The 10-lane bowling alley elevates the sport to new elegance, with Euro bottle service starting at $300. At 9PM it transforms into a black-lit nightclub, where guests can bowl and dance. Weekend DJs spin tunes until 3AM. A must-try: its cotton candy-infused martinis. Post-bowl munchies include burgers, pizza, and deep-fried mac-and-cheese balls.

The **Palms Hotel & Casino (93)** *(4321 W. Flamingo Rd., 702-942-7777 or 866-942-7777, www.palms.com)* offers several interesting nightlife choices. One is **ghostbar (71)** *(702-942-6832, ghostbar-las-vegas.n9negroup.com, daily 8PM–late)*. Atop the tower on the 55th floor, the venue is done up in neon and 1970s space-fantasy decor with an outdoor deck for drinks under the stars and see-through acrylic that provides breathtaking views to the bottom of the hotel. **Rain (72)** *(Palms, 4321 W. Flamingo Rd., 702-942-6832, www.palms.com, daily 11PM–5AM)* is a dance-focused nightclub with all sorts of special effects—fireballs, rain, fountains, and more. Never a dull moment. Front-of-the-line admission is $30. **Tip:** An all-access weekend pass runs $75 per night and includes front-of-the-line admission for one or both clubs. **Moon (73)** *(Palms, 4321 W. Flamingo Rd., 702-942-6832, www.palms.com, daily 10:30PM–late)* is an ultra-lounge above **Playboy** with a huge retractable roof that opens to provide a breathtaking view of the stars and the **Playboy Club**.

WHERE TO SHOP

Malls out-Disney Disney only in Las Vegas. The folks at the **Venetian (82)** call it "streetmosphere" and deliver it in streetscapes lined with delightful destination detail. At the Grand Canal Shoppes (74) *(Venetian, 3355 Las Vegas Blvd. S., monorail stop: Harrah's/Imperial Palace, 702-414-1000, 702-414-4500 or 877-883-6423,*

www.venetian.com), colorful, shallow waterways crossed by romantic step bridges are lined with the facades of Tuscan-toned village residences and shops running the gamut of interests— from **ayurvedic** spa products, to **Jimmy Choo** shoes, to **Murano** glass jewelry, art, and housewares, to Venetian masks—some 80 international boutiques in all. Have a gelato or an Italian ice at St. Mark's Square, sans pigeons. When you're through, rest those tired tootsies and heavy shopping bags in a gondola, and let a costumed gondolier serenade you through the mall on a relaxing, 10-minute float ($15). The new **Palazzo (83)** next door boasts an 85,000-square-foot Barney's New York (75) *(Palazzo, 3325 Las Vegas Blvd. S., monorail stop: Harrah's/Imperial Palace, 702-629-4200, www.barneys.com.)* flagship at **The Shoppes at The Palazzo**, connected to the Venetian (82) via The Grand Canal Shoppes.

Shop like an emperor at the **Forum Shops at Caesars Palace (15)** *(3500 Las Vegas Blvd. S., monorail stop: Flamingo/Caesars Palace, 702-893-4800, www.caesarspalace.com).* This is the Disney-esque mall that started it all when it opened as an ancient Roman metropolis in 1992, complete with a sky of changing hues, an opulent Mediterranean cityscape, gurgling fountains, and animated statuary. Here's where you'll find the Las Vegas addresses for **Escada**, **Gucci**, **Pucci**, **Baccarat**, **Lacroix**, **Valentino**, **Fendi**, **Harry Winston**, and **Kate Spade**, as well as a tri-level **FAO Schwarz** signature store, and refreshment by **Wolfgang Puck**. With 160 boutiques, 13 restaurants, and nearly 700,000 square feet of eye-catching windows and facades, hours can pass easily here. **Tip:** It's a good spot to escape the sun on a hot afternoon.

Via Bellagio (76) *(Bellagio lakeside lobby level promenade, 3600 Las Vegas Blvd. S., monorail stop:*

Bally's/Paris, 702-693-7111 or 888-987-6667, www. bellagio.com) features a corridor of light and Tuscan-style comforts. Marble flooring and cream-colored walls set the stage for about a dozen shops, such as **Tiffany**, **Chanel**, **Dior**, and **Prada**—if it has a home in Paris or Milan, it will be here. Chocoholics can try a new perspective on the sweet stuff at the Jean-Philippe Patisserie (77) *(Bellagio, 3600 Las Vegas Blvd. S. at Flamingo, monorail stop: Bally's/Paris, 702-693-8788, www.bellagio.com, Su–Th 7AM–11PM, F–Sa 7AM–midnight)*. A 27-foot wall seems to pour chocolate—white, light, and dark—right into your senses. The shop, which offers samples on occasion, presents stocked shelves of sweet gold, as well as a counter of candy, desserts, and sandwiches.

Le Boulevard (78) *(3645 Las Vegas Blvd. S., monorail stop: Bally's/Paris, 702-946-7000 or 888-266-5687, www.parislasvegas.com, most shops open 10AM–10PM)* connects **Paris Las Vegas (89)** with **Bally's (86)** via a cobbled promenade of French bistros, shops, and cafés. Its **La Cave** stocks imported cheeses, pâtés, and premium wines. **Les Elements** offers home and garden items. **Presse** is a 24-hour Parisian newsstand.

Around the corner, the Miracle Mile (79) *(3663 Las Vegas Blvd. S., monorail stop: Bally's/Paris, 888-800-8284, www.miracle mileshopslv.com, Su–Th 10AM–11PM, F–Sa 10AM–midnight)* is an actual mile of style with 170 stores and 15 restaurants. Chains include **Victoria's Secret**, **Ann Taylor Loft**, **Chico's**, and **GAP**. Cigar lovers will find rare Cuban-style, hand-rolled varieties at **Havana Republic**. Couples love **ASIA**, a hip Asian-fusion eatery that transforms into a writhing nightclub after the kitchen closes.

WHERE TO STAY

Visiting **Treasure Island Hotel & Casino (80) ($$)** *(3300 Las Vegas Blvd. S. at Spring Mountain Rd., monorail stop: Harrah's/Imperial Palace, then Mirage/Treasure Island tram, running every 10–15 minutes from about 9AM–1AM, 800-944-7444 or 702-894-7111, www. treasureisland.com)* is quite an experience—especially with the *Sirens of TI* (1), its free, front-entrance show (VIP viewing spaces available for guests). For more fun, there's Cirque du Soleil's exotic *Mystère* (2) show and **WET** spa and salon. Every guest gets to enjoy one of the hotel's trademark **Elite SensaTIonal Beds**. With a recent renovation and nearly 3,000 rooms, this is a sleek place to stay. It's also relatively small, and therefore less crowded, than many Strip hotels.

To experience the Strip's original resort-casino, stay at the **Mirage Hotel & Casino (81) ($$)** *(3400 Las Vegas Blvd. S., monorail stop: Harrah's/Imperial Palace, 800-627-6667 or 702-791-7111, www.mirage.com)*. Conceived and built as the Strip's first mega-resort in 1989 by Steve Wynn, its **Volcano (3)** *(see page 85)* erupts with pomp and circumstance four times an hour. This was the first rubbernecker

attraction built right on the Strip. What the hotel hints at outside it delivers within with a semi-real rain forest beneath the lobby dome and a tiger's lair off the lobby. Rooms were recently remodeled with a snappy '60s look. Conveniently located at the Strip's center, with a lush pool area and a fun and contemporary bar scene, the hotel still keeps its edge.

For an unparalleled reminiscence of old Venezia, the place to go is the **Venetian Resort-Hotel-Casino (82) ($$$)** *(3355 Las Vegas Blvd. S. at Sands Ave., monorail stop: Harrah's/Imperial Palace, 877-283-6423 or 702-414-1000, www.venetian.com)*. Plying authentic Venetian canals, gondoliers (some Italian-born) serenade you, and Old World landmarks surround. Boasting 7,000 rooms, the hotel and its **Venezia Tower** represents some of the stateliest digs on the Strip.

Palazzo (83) ($$$) *(3325 Las Vegas Blvd. S., monorail stop: Harrah's/Imperial Palace, 866-263-3001, www.palazzo lasvegas.com.)* is the latest new build in town. In "Vegas think" if you are not expanding, you are falling behind. So the **Venetian (82)** virtually doubled its footprint in 2008 with the opening of its Palazzo, a 3,000-suite, $1.8 billion palace rising 50 stories into the neon. The property brings 450,000 square feet of luxury retail, and more than a dozen new restaurants, including **Carnevino, CUT, Table 10, Morels,** and **Restaurant Charlie** by Charlie Trotter. **Canyon Ranch** doubled its current venue here to become the largest hotel spa in Vegas, if not the country. The exclusive West Coast production of *Jersey Boys* **(12)**

anchors the entertainment, but visitors to this new Stripside behemoth may just wander the grounds, exploring the hotel's 45 pools and fountains and 80-foot glass domes.

The fabulous **Flamingo Las Vegas (84) ($$)** *(3555 Las Vegas Blvd. S., monorail stop: Flamingo/Caesars Palace, 702-733-3111 or 800-732-2111, www.flamingolv.com)* retains little if any of the original edifice that went up here in the desert in 1946. Bugsy Siegel conceived it, built it, opened it, and then died for it months later when the anticipated skim failed to roll in as planned. Today it's part of the Harrah's family. A new redo resulted in a mod retro look; its pink-and-mauve rooms could be part of an *Austin Powers* film. Fifteen center-piece acres of tropical gardens provide peaceful mean-derings amid fountains and koi ponds. **Caesars Palace (85) ($$$)** *(3570 Las Vegas Blvd. S., monorail stop: Flamingo/Caesars Palace, 702-731-7110 or 800-634-6661, www.caesarspalace.com)* is another 1960s hold-out. Simply the most luxurious place on the Strip then, it stays on par with today's competition (**Cleopatra's Barge** still rocks in the late hours, and **Appian Way** is still lined with upscale boutiques designed to catch players in jackpot euphoria). But it's now arrayed with star-chef restaurants, hip clubs, a mineral-bath spa with an arctic cave, a tea sommelier, Swarovski crystal-studded decor, and possibly the most lavish pool in Vegas. The hotel connects at lobby level to the **Forum Shops at Caesars**

Palace (15) *(see page 90)*. Rooms in its **Augustus Tower** are large, quiet, stocked with luxury amenities, and convenient to the check-in desks.

Bally's (86) ($$) *(3645 Las Vegas Blvd. S., monorail stop: Bally's/Paris, 702-739-4111 or 800-634-3434, www. ballyslv.com)* offers large, handsome, comfortable rooms in a convenient center Strip location, with a coffee shop and gourmet Italian restaurant on site. Try the Sunday Sterling brunch. Held ceremoniously in the hotel's steakhouse, it features top entrées as well as all-you-can-eat sushi, caviar, lobster, sturgeon, and a good dozen or two other treats for $65 per person. The pool and spa are small, but the casino is large and connects to Le Boulevard (78), the French-themed shops and bistros of **Paris Las Vegas (89)** next door.

The **Westin Casuarina Las Vegas Hotel, Casino & Spa (87) ($-$$)** *(160 E. Flamingo, monorail stop: Bally's/Paris, 702-836-5900 or 866-837-4215, www.westin.com)* offers quiet lodgings across the street from Bally's. A full-service hotel with a spa, clean rooms, and a small casino, it caters to business travelers and convention attendees. The hotel recently banned smoking; it's one of the few completely nonsmoking hotels in Las Vegas.

Bellagio (88) ($$$) *(3600 Las Vegas Blvd. S., monorail stop: Bally's/Paris, 702-693-7111 or 888-987-6667, www.bellagio.com)* broke the billion-dollar ceiling when it opened in 1998. It was simply the most beautiful, luxurious, and expensive hotel on the Strip, with an army of name chefs from New York, sculptured gardens (in real greenery and glass), a spa that rivals Canyon Ranch as one of the largest hotel spas in the country, über-shopping, and the greatest Cirque show on Earth. Rooms are large, bright, and stocked with amenities usually found in upscale properties. Guests occupying rooms that face the fountains from the 10th floor and above are in for a treat.

Bonjour! **Paris Las Vegas (89)** *($$-$$$) (3655 Las Vegas Blvd. S., monorail stop: Bally's/Paris, 702-946-7000 or 888-266-5687, www.parislasvegas.com)* brings a bit of the Champs-Élysées to the Strip, from twinkle lights in its faux and real trees to its employees' berets and black-and-white striped shirts. Wealth is the word at **Planet Hollywood Resort & Casino (90)** *($$-$$$) (3667 Las Vegas Blvd. S., monorail stop: Bally's/Paris, 702-785-5555 or 866-919-7472, www.planethollywoodresort.com)*, with sleek decor and chandeliers dripping crystal. Starwood account holders accrue loyalty points here, and shoppers like its connected convenience to the **Miracle Mile** mall *(see page 112).* The hip also stay at the **Hard Rock Hotel & Casino (91)** *($$$) (4455 Paradise Rd., monorail stop: Bally's/Paris, 702-693-5000 or 800-473-7625, www.hardrock hotel.com).* A feast for the senses, the hotel appeals to youthful guests with light fixtures made from drum cymbals, a late-night bar and entertainment, a steroidal pool scene (the beach-enclosed lagoon pool features poolside Blackjack), and rock memorabilia throughout—

including genuine Elvis attire, a motorcycle owned by Mötley Crüe, lyrics handwritten by Jim Morrison, and guitars strummed by the biggest names in rock'n'roll. **The Joint** at the hotel is credited with promoting big-name live music performances in Vegas.

Rio (92) ($$) *(3700 W. Flamingo Rd. at Hotel Rio Dr., monorail stop: Harrah's/Imperial Palace, 702-777-7777 or 888-746-7482, www.playrio.com)* promotes its rooms as suites; however, though big, they are simply large rooms. Curved sectional couches are a nice touch and very comfortable, and most rooms have floor-to-ceiling windows. It is possible to get a windowless room, however, so if that is your preference, don't hesitate to ask. Some rooms come with Jacuzzi tubs. Located about a 20-minute walk and a mile west of the Strip, the hotel has two excellent buffets and fun entertainment.

Palms Hotel & Casino (93) ($$-$$$) *(4321 W. Flamingo Rd. at Arville St., monorail stop: Bally's/Paris, 702-942-7777 or 866-725-6773, www.palms.com)* is the place to be if you are young, love to party, and don't mind sleeping off-Strip. MTV films reality shows here, rock bands use the hotel's studio to record, and bachelors rent the **Playboy Club** before the big day. High-end, comfortable beds are larger than average (the hotel's owner also owns a sports team and as such, is sensitive to the needs of taller, bigger persons). Floor-to-

ceiling views over the Las Vegas Valley from the upper stories of the hotel's **Palms and Fantasy Towers** can be heaven (or if you are acrophobic, hell). New **Fantasy Suites** offer pole-dancing rooms, lap-dancing chairs, screening rooms, bowling alleys, basketball courts, round beds with mirrored ceilings, and more.

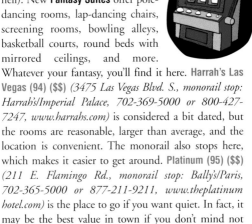

Whatever your fantasy, you'll find it here. **Harrah's Las Vegas (94) ($$)** *(3475 Las Vegas Blvd. S., monorail stop: Harrah's/Imperial Palace, 702-369-5000 or 800-427-7247, www.harrahs.com)* is considered a bit dated, but the rooms are reasonable, larger than average, and the location is convenient. The monorail also stops here, which makes it easier to get around. **Platinum (95) ($$)** *(211 E. Flamingo Rd., monorail stop: Bally's/Paris, 702-365-5000 or 877-211-9211, www.theplatinum hotel.com)* is the place to go if you want quiet. In fact, it may be the best value in town if you don't mind not having a casino in your lobby and a location a block away from the neon. Roomy nonsmoking suites offer modern kitchens, large living, dining, bed, and bath areas, furnished balconies, plasma televisions, and Wi-Fi—all at off-Strip prices.

> "Why don't I just step out and slip into something more spectacular?"
>
> —*Liberace*

chapter 4

SOUTH STRIP

SOUTH STRIP

What to See:

1. Gotham Skyline
2. *Zumanity*
3. Lance Burton
4. Showcase Mall
5. Lion Statue
6. Lion Habitat
7. CBS Television City
8. *KÀ*
9. *La Femme*
10. LIBERACE MUSEUM ★
11. BODIES: The Exhibition
12. *Titanic:* The Artifact Exhibit
13. *Folies Bergere*
14. Tournament of Kings
15. *Thunder Down Under*
16. Pyramid
17. Tomb and Museum of King Tutankhamen
18. IMAX 3–D Theatre
19. *Mamma Mia!*
20. House of Blues
21. Shark Reef

Places to Eat & Drink:

22. Joël Robuchon
23. L'Atelier de Joël Robuchon
24. Shibuya
25. 'Wichcraft
26. Company American Bistro
27. Fusia
28. CatHouse
29. Aureole
30. Fleur de Lys
31. Burger Bar
32. RM Seafood
33. Mix
34. Studio 54
35. Tabu
36. LAX
37. Aurora
38. rumjungle
39. Red Square

Where to Shop:

40. Mandalay Place

Where to Stay:

41. Monte Carlo
42. New York-New York
43. MGM Grand
44. Tropicana
45. Excalibur
46. Luxor
47. Mandalay Bay
48. Four Seasons Las Vegas

★ *Top Picks*

Monorail stop: MGM Grand

Hotel tram between Mandalay Bay, Luxor, and Excalibur

• SNAPSHOT •

The South Strip became the new Center Strip when MGM Grand, New York-New York, Excalibur, Luxor, and Mandalay Bay were constructed in the early- to mid-1990s. In came a roller coaster, a medieval jousting show, a pyramid with tech-heavy attractions and a Nubian motif, and a gleaming golden tower with a pounding wave beach in the back. It looked as if Las Vegas was destined to become a Disney twin. But casino brass found families spent more time with Junior and Sis and less time at the tables than kid-free visitors. So out went the theme parks and in came celebrity chef restaurants, ultra-

lounges, sexy shows, stage productions, and the now-notorious rock'n'roll pool scene. And the city continues to change. Watch for "Manhattanizing" along the Strip as CityCenter, between Bellagio and Monte Carlo, ushers in world-class architecture with Cesar Pelli–designed condominium-hotel high rises and other prestigious properties. What you see today is not what you'll see a year from now.

WHAT TO SEE

It's fun to gawk at the fantastical **Gotham Skyline (1)** across the street at **New York-New York (42)** *(3790 Las Vegas Blvd. S., 702-740-6969 or 800-693-6763, monorail stop: MGM Grand, www.nynyhotelcasino.com).* Admire the **Statue of Liberty** (surrounded by water

and flanked by an NYFD tugboat), the **New York Public Library**, **Empire State** and **Chrysler** buildings, and more. The yellow-and-red **"Manhattan Express" roller coaster** makes for just the right amount of added surrealism. The coaster flies in and out of the hotel at speeds of nearly 70 mph, with 144-foot dives and circular corkscrews, but it's tame enough for most visitors to want to ride again and again *(weekdays 10AM–11PM, weekends 11AM–midnight, weather permitting, $12.50 a ride).* Inside the "Big Apple," **Cirque du Soleil** redefines sexy with *Zumanity* **(2)** *(New York-New York, 3790 Las Vegas Blvd. S., monorail stop: MGM Grand, box office 866-606-7111, www.nynyhotelcasino.com, Tu–W, F–Su 7:30PM and 10:30PM).* Expect an artful, ethereal sequencing of suggestive illusions, nudity, creative comedy, and mesmerizing movement. Tickets are $69 and up, and include sofa seating.

Next door at **Monte Carlo (41)**, **Lance Burton (3)** *(Monte Carlo, 3770 Las Vegas Blvd. S., monorail stop: Bally's/Paris, 877-386-8224 or 702-730-7160, www.monte carlo.com, Tu, Sa 7PM and 10PM, W–F 7PM)* delivers a Las Vegas-style magic show with all the dapper

elegance you'd expect from a master prestidigitator. Tickets cost $66.50 and $72.55.

Walking south along the Strip on the east side of the street, you'll have a hard time missing the **Coca-Cola bottle** that rises more than four stories, accompanied by some seemingly lost **M&M's characters**. This is **Showcase Mall (4)** *(3785 Las Vegas Blvd. S., monorail: MGM Grand, 702-597-3122, hours vary)*, which contains the **World of Coca-Cola Museum**, **M&M's World**, a **Grand Canyon Experience** souvenir store, an Adidas super store, fast food concessions, a **Starbucks**, a **United Artists Cineplex**, and **GameWorks**. Both the Coke and M&M's attractions are sweet fun and free. You'll come across historical, if not sentimental, items here and, in the case of M&M's, a fun 3-D adventure film starring Red and Yellow. At the Coke venue, visitors can sample Coke products for free. **GameWorks** is a Sega-sponsored video arcade packed with old-school favorites like Pac-Man, Centipede, Galaga, Missile Command, pinball machines, air hockey, mechanical-bull riding, and more, plus a rock-climbing wall. The **Grand Canyon Experience** lets you shop for Vegas mugs and T-shirts while periodic thunderstorms erupt.

The largest bronze sculpture in the country is located right here. It's the 45-foot-tall, 50-ton **Lion Statue (5)** *(MGM Grand, 3799 Las Vegas Blvd. S., monorail stop: MGM*  *Grand, 702-891-7777 or 800-929-1111, www.mgm grand.com)*. The golden homage to Metro-Goldwyn-Mayer studio's roaring movie mascot "Leo" watches the world atop a 25-foot pedestal at the corner of the Strip and Tropicana Avenue. Check out the $9 million **Lion Habitat (6)** *(MGM Grand, 3799 Las Vegas Blvd. S., monorail stop: MGM Grand, 702-891-7777 or 800-929-1111, www.mgmgrand.com, free, daily 11AM-10PM)*. Watch kings of beasts curl up like dogs and purr like kittens atop tree branches and rock ledges. Occasionally, a caretaker steps inside to play with or tend to the animals, creating a small show for the viewers. Couch potatoes might like **CBS Television City (7)** *(along Studio Walk at MGM Grand, 3799 Las Vegas Blvd. S., monorail stop: MGM Grand, 702-891-7777 or 800-929-1111, www.mgmgrand.com, free, daily 10AM–10PM)*, where they can watch TV test pilots and register their reactions. Screenings are ongoing, but the process, including surveys and discussions, may take up to 90 minutes. The programs may or may not become content for CBS, Nickelodeon, MTV, and other outlets. A retail shop offers related TV merchandise.

KÀ (8) (MGM Grand, 3799 Las Vegas Blvd. S., monorail stop: MGM Grand, 702-891-7777 or 800-929-1111, www.mgmgrand.com, Tu–Sa at 7PM and 9:30PM) is a true **Cirque du Soleil** masterpiece and its largest show to date. The story line executed in stunning scenes ranging from a dreamy shipwreck and cavalcade of exotic sea creatures to monstrous contraptions and dazzling pyrotechnics. Tickets cost $69 to $150. Ooh-la-lovely *La Femme* (9) *(MGM Grand, 3799 Las Vegas Blvd. S., monorail stop: MGM Grand, 702-891-7777 or 800-929-1111, www.mgmgrand.com, W–M 8PM and 10:30PM)* is a **Crazy Horse** revue direct from the City of Light. Performers were trained on the Paris stage, and numbers range from artful to burlesque. Tickets cost $59 (including four-color program). **Tip**: Ask the box office about packaging shows with dinner at a star-chef hotel restaurant.

Located to the east along Tropicana Avenue, the ★**LIBERACE MUSEUM (10)** *(1775 E. Tropicana Ave. at Spencer, 702-798-5595, www.liberace.com, Tu–Sa 10AM–5PM, Su noon–4PM)* is another attraction you won't find else-

where. Founded in 1979 by the late entertainer's estate, this tribute to "Mr. Showmanship" keeps his spirit and music alive with an astounding collection of gaudy jewelry (home of the world's largest rhinestone), be-gemmed pianos, impressive antiques, unique garments, candelabras, and cars. Decked out in the requisite ruffles and sequins, musician Wes Winters taps out Wladziu Valentino Liberace's greatest hits on a glittering piano *(Tu, W, Sa 1PM)*. Tickets are $17.50, $27.50 for museum and show. Museum-only tickets: $15.00.

Currently at the **Tropicana (44)** itself, blockbuster show **BODIES: The Exhibition (11)** *(Tropicana, 3801 Las Vegas Blvd. S., monorail stop: MGM Grand, box office 800-829-9034, www.tropicanalv.com, daily 10AM–11PM)* presents perfectly preserved specimens of human bodies, showcasing muscles and vascular systems in action, along with stunning vivisections of organs you may not even know you have. Twenty-one examples are on display. Tickets are $29. The fascinating *Titanic*: **The Artifact Exhibit (12)** *(Tropicana, 3801 Las Vegas Blvd. S., monorail stop: MGM Grand, box office 800-829-9034, www.tropicanalv.com, daily 10AM–11PM)* features 300 authentic artifacts discovered 12,500 feet beneath the sea at the final resting place of the famous ship. A replica promenade deck allows you to experience weather conditions like those encountered by the ship's passengers on April 15, 1912. Tickets: $25. Note: At press time, **Luxor (46)** was in negotiation to become the new home of this exhibit. *Folies Bergere* **(13)** *(Tropicana, 3801 Las Vegas Blvd. S., monorail stop: MGM Grand, 800-829-9034, www.tropicanalv.com, Tu and F 8:30PM, M, W, Th, Sa 7:30PM and 10PM)* is the city's longest running (1959) revue of leggy ladies in full plumage, performing everything from the classic can-can to Latin mambo numbers. It's old-school

Vegas at its best—see it while you can (the hotel may soon be in for a complete re-do, if not new build). Seats start at $33.

The **Tournament of Kings (14)** *(Excalibur, 3850 Las Vegas Blvd. S., accessible via MGM Grand monorail stop or Mandalay Bay–Excalibur tram, 702-597-7600, www. excalibur.com, W–M 6PM and 8PM)* is one of the few "dinner shows" left on the Strip, even if cutlery is not included in the deal. Your serving wench will provide plenty of napkins, however, as you watch damsels in distress and handsome knights on horseback joust for their honor. $58.24 inclusive. Buff blokes from Australia take it off during **Thunder Down Under (15)** *(Excalibur, 3850 Las Vegas Blvd. S., accessible via MGM Grand monorail stop or Mandalay Bay–Excalibur tram, 702-597-7600, www.excalibur.com, Su–Th 9PM, F–Sa 9PM and 11PM)*. The gyrating production costs $39.95 (VIP seating $10 more).

The Strip's **Pyramid (16)** *(Luxor, 3900 Las Vegas Blvd. S., accessible via MGM Grand monorail stop or Mandalay Bay–Excalibur tram, 702-262-4444 or 800-288-1000, www.luxor.com)*, dating from AD 1993, remains among the city's most distinctive landmarks. The 30-story, 350-foot pyramid (said to be the largest

in the Western Hemisphere) houses more than 2,500 rooms as well as the world's largest atrium. Within the structure, guests use a 39-degree "inclinator" elevator to reach rooms. At night, a **Skybeam** of light—the planet's most powerful—is projected from the apex of the pyramid. It can be seen from all over Las Vegas and even from space. The guardian **Sphinx** outside is 35 feet taller and 25 feet longer than the original Sphinx in Giza, Egypt. The **Tomb and Museum of King Tutankhamen (17)** *(Luxor, 3900 Las Vegas Blvd. S., accessible via MGM Grand monorail stop or Mandalay Bay–Excalibur tram, 800-963-9364, www.luxor.com,*

10AM–11PM) is an authentic recreation of the tomb of the Egyptian boy king. Self-guided audio tours available. The city's first **IMAX 3-D Theatre (18)** *(Luxor, 3900 Las Vegas Blvd. S., accessible via MGM Grand monorail stop or Mandalay Bay–Excalibur tram, 800-963-9364, www.luxor.com, films shown 10AM–11PM)* offers a variety of stunning, hourlong films projected on a seven-story screen with 30,000 watts of sound. **IMAX Ridefilm** movies feature motion simulator seating.

At **Mandalay Bay (47)**, Celebrated terrarium cum aquarium **Shark Reef (21)** *(Mandalay Bay, 3950 Las Vegas Blvd. S., accessible via MGM Grand monorail stop* or Mandalay Bay–Excalibur tram, 702-632-7777 or 877-632-7000, www.mandalaybay.com, daily 10AM–11PM) descends through four levels of ecology that serve as habitats for crocs, tortoises, monitor lizards, jellyfish, stingrays, horseshoe crabs, and more, before reaching the 1.6 million-gallon tank of salt water that is home to larger predators, including several varieties of shark. A glass tunnel provides an immersive effect. The experience takes about an hour and costs $15.95 for adults. **Mamma Mia! (19)** (Mandalay Bay, 3950 Las Vegas Blvd. S., accessible via MGM Grand monorail stop or Mandalay Bay–Excalibur tram, 702-632-7850, www.mandalaybay.com, Su–Th 7:30PM, Sa 6PM and 10PM) is the ABBA-inspired musical that will have even the most jaded teenager dancing in her seat. This upbeat show deserves every Tony it's earned. Tickets

cost $49.50 to $110. The **House of Blues (20)** (Mandalay Bay, 3950 Las Vegas Blvd. S., 702-632-7600, www.hob.com) brings name stars and comics to an intimate stage. Praise the Lord and pass the biscuits at its legendary **Gospel Sunday Brunch** (702-632-7600, seatings at 10AM and 1PM), $39 adults, $20 children.

PLACES TO EAT & DRINK
Where to Eat:

Las Vegas dining is famed for its contradictions. From buffets aplenty to star-chef menus in star-designer surroundings, from cheap eats to outrageously priced cuisine, from 99-cent shrimp cocktails and nickel cups of coffee (you don't even have to gamble!) to a $5,000 burger, it's all here.

MGM Grand (43) might be considered ground zero for dining along the South Strip, especially with the addition of two restaurants by France's **Joël Robuchon**, "chef of the century." His **Joël Robuchon (22) ($$$)** *(MGM Grand, 3799 Las Vegas Blvd. S., monorail stop: MGM Grand, 702-891-7777 or 800-929-1111, www.mgmgrand.com, F–Sa 5:30PM–10:30PM, S–Th 5:30PM–10PM, formal dress, limited seating)* (formerly Joël Robuchon at The Mansion), is where you'll discover six- and 16-course tasting menus (priced at $225 and $360 per person, respectively) that offer the dining experience of a lifetime. Next door, **L'Atelier de Joël Robuchon (23) ($$$)** *(MGM Grand, 3799 Las Vegas Blvd. S., monorail stop: MGM Grand, 702-891-7777 or 800-929-1111, www.mgmgrand.com, Su–Th 5PM–10:30PM, F–Sa 5PM–11:30PM, business casual, limited seating)* offers tapas and small plates gorgeously presented at a bar, with an open kitchen behind. The tiny venue makes for communal dining, but every bite is a treat. Checks average $125 per person with paired wine. Test your sake acumen at stunning **Shibuya (24) ($$$)** *(MGM Grand, 3799 Las Vegas Blvd. S., monorail stop: MGM Grand, 702-891-3001, www.mgmgrand.com, Su–Th 5PM–10PM, F–Sa 10AM–8PM)*. Things can get frenetic at this high-energy, Tokyo-style establishment, offering sushi, sashimi, and Japanese seafood compositions. But after the sake sommelier shows up, you won't feel a

thing. Signature dishes include toro tartare, miso wild salmon, and kampachi with fresh yuzu and black truffle oil. Checks average $75 per person. Casual and eat-and-run diners won't do better than 'Wichcraft (25) ($) *(MGM Grand, 3799 Las Vegas Blvd. S., monorail stop: MGM Grand, 702-891-3001, www.mgmgrand.com, Su–Th 10AM–6PM, F–Sa 10AM–8PM)*. Here New York star chef **Tom Colicchio**, who is also at the helm of the hotel's noted **Craftsteak ($$$)** restaurant, prepares food for the rest of us, featuring fresh artisanal breads and slow-roasted meats, like roasted pork loin with red cabbage, jalapeños, and mustard on ciabatta roll, or Sicilian tuna with fennel, black olives, and lemon on baguette. **Tip**: The breakfast pastries are some of the best in town.

The newly refurbished **Luxor (46)** has replaced excessive Egyptian ambience with an adult contemporary experience through a phalanx of unusual "it" clubs and restaurants. **Company American Bistro (26) ($$-$$$)** *(Luxor, 3900 Las Vegas Blvd. S., accessible via MGM Grand monorail stop or Mandalay Bay–Excalibur tram, 702-262-4444, www.luxor.com, Tu–Sa 5:30PM–midnight, lounge W–Sa 5:30PM–4AM)* reinvents the concept of the American bistro within a 10,000-square-foot fireside lodge created by investors Nicky Hilton, Nick Lachey, and Wilmer Valderrama. The Asian-inspired, larger-portion appetizer menu at **Fusia (27) ($$)** *(Luxor, 3900*

Las Vegas Blvd, S., 702-262-4778, wwwluxor.com, daily 6PM–11PM) is meant for sharing. Try the blue crab and rock shrimp rolls or macadamia nut-glazed chicken. Then there is **CatHouse (28) ($$-$$$)** *(Luxor, 3900 Las Vegas Blvd. S., accessible via MGM Grand monorail stop or Mandalay Bay–Excalibur tram, 702-262-4702, wwwluxor.com)*—both a sexy restaurant *(daily 5PM–11PM)* and European ultra-lounge *(M, F, Sa 10PM–close)* that invokes a 19th-century French bordello with voyeuristic visuals and provocatively attired staff. Low-light chandeliers, tufted fabric walls, and a cobalt blue color scheme provide a sultry backdrop for star chef **Kerry Simon**'s tapas-style plates.

Charlie Palmer's **Aureole (29) ($$$)** *(Mandalay Bay, 3950 Las Vegas Blvd. S., accessible via MGM Grand monorail stop or Mandalay Bay–Excalibur tram, 702-632-7777 or 877-632-7000, www.aureolelv.com, dinner Su–Th 6PM–10:30PM, F–Sa 5:30PM–10:30PM, wine lounge open 6PM–12AM)* helped launch the celebrity chef movement in Las Vegas. It's famous for its Adam Tihany–designed interior and bar-none, four-story wine tower navigated by "wine angels"—lithe, black-clad women who rappel up and down the tower retrieving requested labels. The menu features interpretive American cuisine (think sea scallop sandwiches in crisp potato crust or wood-fired filet mignon with Cabernet sauce). Prix-fixe menus come in three- and seven-course options ($75 and $95 respectively) before wine pairings. **Fleur de Lys (30) ($$$)** *(Mandalay Bay, 3950 Las Vegas Blvd. S., accessible via MGM Grand monorail stop or Mandalay Bay–Excalibur tram, 702-632-7777 or 877-632-7000, www.mandalaybay.com 5:30PM–10:30PM daily)* brings San Francisco chef **Hubert Keller**'s expertise to the Strip with a dark, cavernous room filled with lavish floral sculptures and fine French cuisine. Recommended dessert: peach mousse cake, served with champagne sorbet. Tasting menus start at $74, adding $50 for wine pairing. Or you can opt for the $5,000 Kobe beef burger (and fries, of course). It comes with a bottle of 1990 Château Pétrus. For a taste of this Alsace-born, Bocuse-trained chef's talents without sticker shock, try **Burger Bar (31) ($-$$)** *(Mandalay Place retail promenade,*

3950 Las Vegas Blvd. S., accessible via MGM Grand monorail stop or Mandalay Bay–Excalibur tram, 702-632-9364, www.mandalay bay.com, M–Th 10:30AM–11PM, F 10:30AM–2AM, Sa 10AM–2AM, Su 10AM–11PM). Here you can have fabulous beef, turkey, or even garden burgers topped with any of more than 40 items—all available for under $10, or try the ultimate Rossini burger ($60) with the eatery's famous Madeira wine sauce. More than a burger joint, you'll find designer fries here, too, plus two dozen international beers on tap, and all manner of shakes, floats, and even "dessert burgers."

Seafood in the desert should be left to the pros, like **Rick Moonen**. His **RM Seafood (32)** *(Mandalay Place entrance, 3930 Las Vegas Blvd. S., accessible via MGM Grand monorail stop or Mandalay Bay–Excalibur tram, 702-632-9300, www.rmseafood.com, 5PM–10:30PM)* gets the awards and the attention. Rick is committed to

using sustainably caught seafood and organically grown, sustainable produce. His venue is actually two restaurants: **RM Upstairs ($$$)**, a fine-dining space with glass-and-wood appointments resembling a yacht, serves items like lobster bisque followed by Alaskan halibut with lobster ravioli, caramelized mushrooms, and sauce Bercy. Seven-course prix-fixe menu available for $135. **RM Downstairs ($-$$)** is more casual; think flavorful clam chowder and Anchor Steam-battered fish and chips. There's an elaborate sushi menu here, too. Note: Moonen loves using yuzu in his recipes.

For the views if not the haute dining experience, **Alain Ducasse's Mix (33) ($$$)** *(THEhotel at Mandalay Bay, accessible via MGM Grand monorail stop or Mandalay Bay–Excalibur tram, 64th floor, 3950 Las Vegas Blvd. S., 702-632-9500, www.chinagrillmgt.com/mixlv, nightly 6PM–11PM)* should not be missed. The sprawling white space makes you feel as if you're in a champagne bubble above the neon. The sensation is enhanced by a collection of no less than 15,000 hand-blown Murano glass spheres of the chandelier that serves as the focal point for the retro white-and-silver room. Views within and without will be forgotten quickly once the food appears, however—maestro Ducasse holds three Michelin stars in three different countries. The menu here reflects his passion for comfort foods: bison tenderloin sauce *au poivre* with a mix of vegetables; elbow pasta with black truffle, ham, gruyere cheese; Dungeness crab salad with Granny Smith apple-and-cucumber "gelee," and, for dessert, maple syrup tiramisu or homemade ice cream. Entrées run $32 to $75, and every bite is worth its weight in caloric gold. Take in some of the best views of the city at the adjoining **Mix Lounge**, where the outdoor terrace allows you to take in the stars . . . and the celebs.

Bars & Nightlife:

The 1970s-style **Studio 54 (34)** *(MGM Grand, 3799 Las Vegas Blvd. S., monorail stop: MGM Grand, 702-891-7254, www.mgmgrand.com, Tu–Sa 10PM–close)* reincarnation might be fun if you enjoy go-go girls egging on your dance moves. The mammoth venue, complete with four dance floors and wall walkers, is perhaps more popular with the over-30 crowd than ultra-lounge **Tabu (35)** *(MGM Grand, 3799 Las Vegas Blvd. S., monorail stop: MGM Grand, 702-891-7183, www.tabulv.com, Th–M 10PM–close)*. Here you're certain to spend time in front of the velvet rope, but, once in, you'll love the high-tech visual effects. Both spots have VIP lounges where you can spend well over $1,000 for a bottle and a stogie.

The sexy new scene inside the pyramid includes **LAX (36)** *(Luxor, 3900 Las Vegas Blvd. S., accessible via MGM*

Grand monorail stop or Mandalay Bay–Excalibur tram, 702-4529, www.luxor.com, W–Su 10PM–close), a DJ nightclub that attracts Paris Hilton adherents (as well as the socialite herself) with pulsing, two-story dance spaces and VIP bottle-service cubbies. Sister club **Noir Bar** *(Luxor, 3900 Las Vegas Blvd. S., accessible via MGM Grand monorail stop or Mandalay Bay–Excalibur tram, W–Su 10PM–close)* raises the bar; this small, exclusive room (within **LAX**) has a private, hidden entrance open only to those whose names are on the elite guest list or who know the password. Once in, you follow a passageway to a candlelit speakeasy appointed in leather and crystal. **Aurora (37)** *(Luxor, 3900 Las Vegas Blvd. S., accessible via MGM Grand monorail stop or Mandalay Bay–Excalibur tram, 702-262-4591, wwwluxor.com, daily 24 hours)* is another atmospheric hot spot. Evoking nature's Northern Lights phenomenon, this striking, 157-seat lounge was designed by Japanese firm Super Potato. Martinis, mojitos, and margaritas are the thing here. The provocative **CatHouse (28)** *(see page 133)* morphs from restaurant to ultra-lounge *(M, F–Sa 10PM–close)*, boasting duo DJs spinning mainstream dance and European vocal house, complemented by lingerie-clad dancers.

rumjungle (38) *(Mandalay Bay, 3950 Las Vegas Blvd. S., accessible via MGM Grand monorail stop or Mandalay Bay–Excalibur tram, 702-632-7408, www.mandalay bay.com, M, W, F–Sa 11PM–4AM, Tu, Th, Su 11PM–2AM)* is a rowdy, crowded, frenetic scene that combines the world's largest rum bar with pyrotech-

nics and trapeze artists that entertain from above. Evoking a 19th-century Bolshevik salon, **Red Square (39)** *(Mandalay Bay, 3950 Las Vegas Blvd. S., accessible via MGM Grand monorail stop or Mandalay Bay–Excalibur tram, 702-632-7407, Su–Th 5PM–2AM, F 5PM–4AM, Sa 3PM–4AM)* is a kick. A decapitated statue of Russian revolutionary Vladimir Lenin fronts the place (the head was stolen a few years back, but no one seems to mind). Sip a Stoli martini with a blue-cheese-stuffed olive on the (real) ice bar. Down rare vodkas in the ice locker (fur coats and hats provided by the management).

WHERE TO SHOP

The Mandalay Place (40) *(bet. Mandalay Bay and Luxor, 3950 Las Vegas Blvd. S., 702-632-7777, most shops open 10AM–11PM)* packs in plenty of shopportunities. **Maude** is for all the fashionistas who like hip, but affordable clothes for $100 or less. The 100,000-square-foot sky bridge also houses **Urban Outfitters**, **Lik Design**, **GF Ferré**, **Fornarina**, **Davidoff**, **Nike Golf**, **Oilily**, **Cavalli**. Must-see shops include **Lush Puppy** for fashionable pet gear and **55 Degrees Wine + Design** *(702-632-9355, wine tastings F 3PM–6PM)*, from the team that brought you the wine tower at **Aureole (29)** *(see page 133)*.

WHERE TO STAY

You'll find the resort hotels along the South Strip offer clean, comfortable standard rooms (albeit some with more amenities than others), congested casinos, a myriad of dining choices, expensive cocktail lounges staffed by carefully groomed hostesses, and world-class entertainment. Many consider **Monte Carlo (41) ($-$$)** *(3770 Las Vegas Blvd. S., monorail stop: Bally's/Paris, 702-730-7777 or 800-311-8999, www.montecarlo.com)* one of the best values around. Accommodations can be upgraded to concierge level with all privileges for an added $50 a night. **New York-New York (42) ($-$$)** *(3790 Las Vegas Blvd. S., monorail stop: MGM Grand, 702-740-6969 or 800-689-1797, www.nynyhotelcasino.com)* fascinates guests with its mini **Central Park**, cute **Greenwich Village**, and kid-pleasing **Coney Island midway**. The baby Big Apple connects via skywalk to **MGM Grand (43) ($$-$$$)** *(3799 Las Vegas Blvd. S., monorail stop: MGM Grand, 702-891-7777 or 877-880-0880, www.mgmgrand.com)*, one of the largest hotels in the world. (Expect to get lost here at least once.) Its six-acre **Grand Pool Complex** *(702-891-3086)* includes a 10-minute river ride. At the top of the lion? Luxurious **Skylofts ($$$)** *(3799 Las Vegas Blvd. S., 877-646-5638, www.skyloftsmgmgrand.com)*, two-story boutique lodgings designed by architect Tony Chi. Amenities/services include infinity-edged spa tubs, Jura espresso/coffee machines, preferred restaurant seating, and "Dream Butler" service. Also connected to the hotel: **The Signature ($$-$$$)** *(145 E. Harmon Ave., 877-612-2121, www.signaturemgmgrand.com)*, offering junior, one-, and two-bedroom no-gaming suites that combine the conveniences of hotel services with a separate gated entrance and private pool area.

For classic Vegas, try the **Tropicana (44) ($)** *(3801 Las Vegas Blvd. S., monorail stop: MGM Grand, 702-739-2222 or 888-826-8767, www.tropicanalv.com)*. Its expansive **Lagoon Pool**—lushly landscaped with trees, plants, and flowers—is one of the original outside-the-box pool designs in the city. Swim-up Blackjack tables are equipped with heated drop boxes to dry damp bills. Across the street at **Excalibur (45) ($)** *(3850 Las Vegas Blvd. S., accessible via MGM Grand monorail stop or Mandalay Bay–Excalibur tram, 702-597-7777 or 877-750-5464, www.excalibur.com)*, rooms are under renovation. Out is the Camelot look; in is an edgy style *GQ* might applaud. The pool area is being upgraded to offer twice as much swimming and lounging space, with both scene and scenery. **Luxor (46) ($-$$)** *(3900 Las Vegas Blvd. S., accessible via MGM Grand monorail stop or Mandalay Bay–Excalibur tram, 702-262-4444 or 888-777-0188, www.luxor.com)* is being refurbished as well, with excessive Egyptian ambience being phased out and an adult contemporary experience being ushered in. New attractions inside the pyramid will include a **Cirque du Soleil** premiere featuring the revolutionary illusions of **Criss Angel**. **Mandalay Bay (47) ($$-$$$)** *(3950 Las Vegas Blvd. S., accessible via MGM Grand monorail stop or Mandalay Bay–Excalibur tram, 702-632-7777 or 877-632-7800, www.mandalaybay.com)* maintains a South Seas appeal with large, upscale rooms and a lavish 11-acre pool complex; here, Euro bathing draws the over-21 set, families prefer wave-breaking waters beneath faux ruins, and gamers go for the recent beach/casino addition that opens onto the pool. The resort's no-gaming **THEHotel ($$$)**, with its large, handsome suites, is favored by families and business travelers. **Four Seasons Las Vegas (48) ($$$)** *(top four floors of Mandalay Bay, 3960 Las Vegas Blvd. S., accessible via MGM Grand monorail stop or Mandalay Bay–Excalibur tram, 702-632-5000 or 877-632-5000, www.four seasons.com/lasvegas)* is another hotel-within-a-hotel set-up. Its exclusive pool area is a draw. Both connect via a corridor to **Mandalay Bay (47)**.

"Vegas, baby! Vegas!"

—*Swingers (1996)*

chapter 5

BEYOND THE NEON

BEYOND THE NEON

What to See:

1. Springs Preserve
2. RED ROCK CANYON ★
3. Bonnie Springs Ranch
4. Blue Diamond
5. Pahrump
6. Pahrump Valley Winery
7. Death Valley
8. Mt. Charleston
9. Las Vegas Motor Speedway
10. VALLEY OF FIRE STATE PARK ★
11. Lost City Museum of Archaeology
12. Mesquite
13. Zion National Park
14. Lake Las Vegas
15. MonteLago Village
16. Lake Mead National Recreation Area
17. Boulder City
18. Hoover Dam Museum
19. HOOVER DAM ★
20. Black Canyon
21. GRAND CANYON ★

Places to Eat & Drink:

22. Little A'Le'Inn
23. Feast Buffet at Sunset Station
24. The Feast Around the World Buffet at Green Valley Ranch Resort
25. The Feast Buffet at Red Rock Casino Resort Spa
26. The Original Pancake House
27. T-Bones Chophouse
28. Salt Lick Bar B-Q
29. Ceres
30. Spiedini Ristorante
31. Gustav Mauler Cigar Lounge
32. Vintner Grill
33. Rosemary's Restaurant
34. Bistro Zinc
35. Whiskey Bar
36. Cherry
37. Dylan's Dance Hall and Saloon
38. Dew Drop Inn
39. Four Mile Bar
40. Dick's Tavern
41. Kahootz Bar
42. The Railhead

★ *Top Picks*

"We were stark mad with excitement, drunk with happiness, smothered under mountains of prospective wealth."

—*Mark Twain, on visiting Nevada*

BEYOND THE NEON

West to Death Valley, South to Primm,
North to Zion, East to Hoover Dam

• SNAPSHOT •

There is nothing like the commotion of the Strip—the nonstop pulsing of casino lights, throb of rock music, clanging of slot machines, screams of lucky winners, groans of those who've lost, and reverberations of entertainers belting out numbers from countless lounge stages. You feel as though you're at the epicenter of the universe, with something important happening every minute. And it's not until you escape the clutches of this seductive whirlwind that you experience the Vegas gift few visitors find—the pure silence of the majestic desert expanse surrounding the city. Getting into Las Vegas means getting out of Las Vegas, too. The nature of the city is go, go, go. The nature around the city makes you want to stop, simply stop. The nature of your holiday? Having it all.

Nevada's rough country was home to the ancient Anasazi and the Paiutes in later centuries. Remnants of these civilizations are still reflected in the stone of the national and state

park systems near Las Vegas. Just twenty minutes from the Strip, you'll discover Red Rock Canyon, offering a tranquil loop through stunning ferriferous rock formations. Get out of the car, walk down a well-mapped path, and you're suddenly more alone than you could have ever imagined, intensely aware of every puff of breeze or "caw" of a crow. This is a land of adventure, to be explored by hiking, mountain biking, horseback riding, kayaking, and pontooning.

Mysterious discoveries await as well. The desert near Red Rock and points beyond has long been considered by some a landing pad for extraterrestrial saucers. Death Valley offers all sorts of strange phenomena as well, including large rocks that appear to have slid across the floor of ancient lakebeds under their own steam.

Resorts outside Las Vegas are relaxing, rejuvenating destinations. Here the pull to see and do succumbs to the simpler pleasures of taking in the mountain scenery and listening to nature's healing stillness.

WHAT TO SEE

Heading west from the Strip, you'll come across **Springs Preserve (1)** *(333 S. Valley View Blvd. at Alta Dr., 702-822-7700, www.springspreserve.org, open daily 10AM– 6PM)*, a 180-acre cultural and historic site with museums, galleries, events, educational and play opportunities for children, interpretive trails, a botanical garden, and the future **Nevada State Museum** *(opening 2009)*. The excellent exhibits here include a live bat lair and halls focused on recycling, environmental preservation, and cutting-edge, sustainable building construction methods. You can also experience a **simulated flash flood**, complete with 5,000 gallons of water! Adult admission is $18.95.

★RED ROCK CANYON (2) *(W. Charleston Blvd. to Rt. 159, follow Rt. 159 to canyon entrance, www.redrockcanyonlv.org, open daily 6AM–dusk)* offers a peaceful, one-
way loop that runs 13 miles through stunning rock formations with fiery hues. Start with the worthwhile **Bureau of Land Management Visitor Center** *(at the entrance, 702-515-5350)* that explains the canyon's natural history, provides maps, and details 23 marked trails on and off the route. The sandstone markings reveal the geologic drama of roiling rivers that once zigzagged the landscape. Petroglyphs dot the **Willow Springs** trails. In cool weather, small waterfalls plunge from 1,000-foot sandstone heights at the end of the **Ice Box Canyon** trail. The fee for a scenic drive is $5. Mountain bikes are not permitted, but pets are

(with leashes, baggies, and water). Guided horseback tours are available through **Cowboy Trail Rides** *(702-387-2457, www.cowboytrailrides.com)*.

After your drive, take the long way back to town and turn right instead of left for **Bonnie Springs Ranch (3)** *(1 Gunfighter Ln.,*

702-875-4191, www.bonnie springs.com). The ranch is about two miles down on the right; take the road to the parking area. This former watering hole for wagon trains and a cattle ranch in the mid-1800s now has a free petting and wildlife zoo, an aviary, and bullpen. The ranch's **Old Nevada** is a replica of an Old West town, with a general store, blacksmith shop, opera house, chapel, and a saloon. Stop here for post-Red Rock hike refreshments: beer in summer and hot chocolate in winter. It's also the place for burgers and good times on weekend nights.

Another mile down the road, discover **Blue Diamond (4)** *(Blue Diamond Rd., Rt. 159)* a quiet hamlet built in the 1940s for executives and workers in a gypsum mine nearby. It's not quite an attraction, but with its general store, library, and postmaster who knows everyone's name (and life story), it does offer a nostalgic glimpse into the past. The wild descendants of burros once used by itinerant gold miners have the run of the streets. This picturesque town is a great spot to sit, have a Popsicle, and watch the world go by.

Continue on until you reach the intersection of Route 160. Go left or east and take it back to Las Vegas. Take a right or go west and head about 60 miles until

you reach **Pahrump (5)** through the scenic **Spring Mountains National Recreation Area** and **Mt. Potosi,** (the site of the plane crash that claimed the life of 1930s actress Carole Lombard). Don't blink or you might miss the town known best for its cathouses (it's just over the county line in **Nye County,** where prostitution is legal). The infamous **Chicken Ranch** and **Sheri's Ranch** are long-time operations here; Heidi Fleiss is said to be building a spot that will cater to women. This expanding community, also the home of talk radio broadcaster **Art Bell,** is said to have a UFO center in the works. The nearby **Pahrump Valley Winery (6)** *(3810 Winery Rd., 800-368-9463 or 775-751-7800, www.pahrumpwinery.com)* makes a fine day trip. And OK, most of the grapes come from and are bottled in California, but the label is all Pahrump. On the Mission-styled site, you'll find a tasting room, gift shop, and **Symphony's** (an elegant restaurant with views of the desert foothills), plus jazz concerts, dancing, and picnics under the stars.

Take Route 160 north to Highway 95 and follow the signs to **Death Valley (7)** *(about a two-hour drive from Las Vegas).* This is the lowest point in the Western Hemisphere, around 300 feet below sea level. History buffs love the Death Valley area. Here's where 20-mule teams transported the mineral borax 165 miles from desert mines to the railroad in the 1880s, and where pioneers endured untold desert

 hardships in their attempts to reach the coast. Expect discussions about the odd flora and fauna that flourish in this tough clime, the mysterious rocks and boulders that "slide" across the floor of the region's secluded Racetrack Playa, and about the region's extreme temperatures (it reached 134 degrees here in 1913, topped only by 136 degrees in Libya in 1922). In winter, however, the weather is fine, making a stay at the **Furnace Creek Inn** and **Furnace Creek Ranch Resort (45)** *(Hwy. 190, 760-786-2345, www.furnace creekresort.com)* a unique treat indeed. The inn **($$$)** offers comfy, four-diamond accommodations; the ranch **($-$$)** is more budget- and family-oriented. Note: The inn is closed from May through October. Lodgings here feature swimming pools that make use of the area's warm mineral waters. Guest of the inn may slip into a robe after a hot soak, relax on a private veranda, and watch the stars.

The 12,000-foot **Mt. Charleston (8)** *(off Hwy. 95 north to the Hwy. 157 turnoff)*, a pleasant 45-minute drive north of the Strip, beckons in summer with cooler temperatures and the restful **Humboldt-Toiyabe National Forest**; this might be the easiest and most rewarding of afternoon excursions. Halfway up, the **Hotel on Mount Charleston (46) ($$$)** *(2 Kyle Canyon Rd., 702-872-5500, www.mtcharlestonhotel.com)*, a mid-1970s-style lodge, offers rooms with views of the valley, private terraces, feather beds, and (electric) fireplaces. You can have a wedding here, or rent horses for tours of the terrain. They also boast a state-of-the-art health and wellness spa. Continue up the mountain to **Mount Charleston Lodge (47) ($$)** *(1200 Old Park Rd., 702-872-5408 or 800-955-1314, www.mtcharlestonlodge.com)*, where the weather is as much as 30 degrees cooler than in town. Enjoy sweeping views, the glint of aspen leaves, the scent of Ponderosa pines, and in winter, the warmth of a crackling wood fire. The hiking is sublime, with well-marked trails that lead past waterfalls to rewarding vistas spanning 100 miles. In the fall, the colors turn gold and red. The road loops around to meet  Highways 158 and 156, which snake through **Kyle Canyon** and the **Lee Canyon Ski Resort** *(702-385-2754, www.skilasvegas.com)*.

The crowd-pleasing **Las Vegas Motor Speedway (9)** *(7000 Las Vegas Blvd. N., take I-15 north about 12 miles from Downtown Las Vegas to Speedway Exit 54, 800-644-4444, www.lvms.com)* is among the world's leading-edge racing facilities, with a super speedway, an International Automobile Federation (FIA)–sanctioned road course, a drag strip, short-track ovals, driving schools, motocross, go-kart, and other attractions and events for all ages.

TOP PICK!

Go back—way back—in time at the ★**VALLEY OF FIRE STATE PARK (10)** (*Interstate 15, 702-397-2088, www.parks.nv.gov, open year-round 8:30AM–4:30PM*), 50 miles northeast of Las Vegas. This is Nevada's oldest and largest (36,000 acres) state park. It derives its name from the vivid purple-red sandstone formations created 150 million years ago; they appear to be on fire when they reflect the sun's rays. Many science fiction filmmakers have used this other-worldly area as a setting for their movies. (Captain Kirk lost his life here in *Star Trek: Generations*). Start at the **Visitors Center**, which has displays on the park's history, ecology, and archaeology. Two of the most interesting formations to look out for are **Elephant Rock** and **Seven Sisters**. Wander **Petroglyph Canyon Trail**, where you'll discover 3,000-year-old Indian markings. Want more information? Visit the **Lost City Museum of Archaeology (11)** in the nearby town of Overton (*721 S. Moapa Valley Blvd., 702-397-2193, www.comnettnet, daily 8:30AM–4:30PM*).

Highway 93 on the way to **Overton** will take you toward the **Nevada Test Site** and **Extraterrestrial Highway** (*Hwy. 375*), so named because it skirts the legendary Area 51 and is believed to be a magnet for Earth-bound UFOs. Stop by **Little A'Le'Inn (22)** (*1 Old Mill Rd., 775-729-2515, www.littlealeinn.com, daily 8AM–10PM*) in the tiny town of **Rachel** for a burger that is "out of this world." Old mines and ghost towns dot the landscape of this lonely 98-mile stretch. Keep your camera ready for an ET sighting.

Interstate 15 past Overton leads to **Mesquite (12)**, a

spread of alfalfa farms and ranches 80 miles from Las Vegas; it's trying to become a resort satellite with golf, casinos, entertainment, and spa hotels. The top venues here are **CasaBlanca Resort, Casino, Golf & Spa (48) ($)** *(950 W. Mesquite Blvd., 702-346-7529 or 1-877-GETAWAY, www.casablanca resort.com)* and the **Oasis Resort,**

Casino, Golf & Spa (49) ($) *(897 W. Mesquite Blvd., 702-346-5232 or 1-877-GETAWAY, www.oasisresort.com)*. Both have standard hotel accommodations at bottom rates with meandering pools and separate spa facilities. Golf is arranged at the **Palms Golf Club** *(711 Palms Blvd., 866-401-6020, www.palmsgolfclub.com)*, a championship course with a mountainous back nine. Other recreational attractions here include shooting, compliments of the **Oasis Gun Club** *(897 W. Mesquite Blvd., 702-346-5232),* where skeet, sports, and

range shooting enthusiasts are accommodated. Or take the skydiving plunge through **Skydive Mesquite** *(1200 Kittyhawk Dr., 877-246-5867, www.skydive mesquite.com)*.

But hiking and sightseeing are the biggest draws for visitors en route to Utah's **Zion National Park (13)** *(Hwy. 9 near Springdale, 435-772-3256, www.nps.gov/zion)*, about three hours from Vegas. The sandstone spectacle here blends rose-colored hues with browns, siennas, beiges, and whites; the landscape rises 2,000 feet in river-carved, weather-swept formations above the scrub-forested basin, which also includes creeks, rivers, and water-hewn arches in the backcountry. You'll find plenty of trails for hiking, biking, bird-watching, and photography. Maps and schedules of ranger-led activities can be obtained at the visitors' center. Fees are steep—$25 per car (but it's a seven-day pass); extra fees are charged to proceed through certain parts of the park.

Heading east from the Strip? Seventeen miles out, you'll come across **Lake Las Vegas (14)** *(1600 Lake Las Vegas Pkwy., Henderson, 702-564-1600 or 800-564-1603, www.lakelasvegas.com)*. Developers diverted water from Lake Mead to create this 320-acre lake, then built resorts, golf courses, million-dollar homes, and a picture-perfect village. It does make a serene alternative to the tumult of Vegas. Two hotel properties—**Ritz-Carlton, Lake Las Vegas (50)** *(1610 Lake Las Vegas Pkwy., Henderson, 702-567-4700, www.ritzcarlton.com)* and **Loews Lake Las Vegas Resort (51)** *(101 MonteLago Blvd., Henderson, 702-567-6000 or 877-285-6397, www.loews hotels.com)*—offer top accommodations. A third property—**MonteLago Village Resort (52)** *(1600 Lake Las Vegas Pkwy., Henderson, 702-564-4700 or 866-564-4799, www.MonteLagovillage.com)*—offers condo/hotel accommodations with living areas, kitchens, and balconies. The area's focal point is **MonteLago Village (15)**, a re-creation of a lakeside Italian fishing hamlet with Tuscan facades, cobbled pedestrian promenades, bistro dining, star-chef culinary experiences, chic home, clothing, and art shops and galleries. The village hosts weekend events, including art fairs, evening concerts on the lake, jazz under the stars, and wine walks.

A little further out, you'll find **Lake Mead National Recreation Area (16)**. Take Lake Shore Drive to the **Alan Bible Visitor Center** *(Rt. 93 W. and Lakeshore Scenic Dr., 702-293-8990, www.nps.gov/lame, daily 8:30AM–4:30PM, closed New Year's Day, Thanksgiving, Christmas)* to get an orientation. The water is warm, muddy, and not really suitable for swimming, although there are beaches. And unless you're ready to commission a yacht or houseboat, the best way to see the lake is by paddle-wheeler. **Lake Mead Cruises** *(702-293-6180, www.lakemeadcruises.com)* runs sightseeing and meal cruises all year, with Mississippi-style paddle-wheelers that carry 300 passengers on three decks. Cruises start at $22 for adults and $10 for children.

The town of **Boulder City (17)** *(www.bcnv.org, Parks and Recreation Dept., 900 Arizona St., Boulder City, 702-293-9256, open M–Th 7AM–6PM; F 9AM–noon, 1PM–5PM)*, eight miles west of **Hoover Dam (19)** *(see page 156)* was built for both the construction brass and the muscle which constructed the engineering marvel. You won't find casinos here, just a diner or two, a rock shop, and other notion stores. But the restored 1933 **Boulder Dam Hotel (53) ($)** *(1305 Arizona St., Boulder City, 702-293-3510, www.boulderdamhotel.com)* houses the worthwhile **Hoover Dam Museum (18)** *(1305 Arizona St., Boulder City, 702-294-1988, www.bcmha.org, M–Sa 10AM–5PM, Su noon–5PM, closed New Year's Day, Easter, Mother's Day, Thanksgiving, Christmas)*, which provides an excellent opportunity to explore the town's past. It features photographs, artifacts, oral histories, and even recorded sounds of the dam's construction echoing off the walls of Black Canyon. Visitors really get a feel for the complexity, danger, and scale of the mammoth project.

Vegas is known for crowd-stopping attractions, but just a 40-minute drive away, you'll discover the stunner that is still considered one of the seven man-made wonders of the modern world As you wend your way through colossal geologic canyon formations, the approach to ★**HOOVER DAM (19)** *(Rt. 83, 702-494-2517 or 866-730-9097, www.usbr.gov/lc/hooverdam, open daily 9AM–5PM, except Thanksgiving and Christmas)* is as riveting as the structure itself. Behemoth electric cable towers jut from the rocks at odd angles in a surrealistic setting perhaps more appropriate for a mid-century Japanese sci-fi flick. A million people a year take the tour. Parking costs $7 *(cash only)* and the tour costs $11 for adults and $9 for kids *(ages 4–16)*. The air-conditioned visitor center displays murals, maps, and photos as an introduction to dam history, plus a film describing how engineering feats through history tamed the mighty Colorado. You then take large elevators 500 feet down and walk through a 250-foot-long tunnel drilled out of rock to

TOP PICK!

view the 650-foot-long Nevada power plant wing and its massive turbine generators. See four 30-foot-diameter pipes transporting nearly 90,000 gallons of water per second from Lake Mead to the hydroelectric generators in the powerhouse, and get a panoramic view of the lake and Colorado River from an observation room. The concrete structure, which is 600 feet thick at its base and extends for 54 stories, is said to be haunted by ghosts of some of the 96 men who lost their lives during the dam's construction between 1930 and 1935. It has also been a suicide spot over the years. **Tip:** Despite soaring temperatures in summer, this is when the dam is most crowded (it's also crowded

during spring break season). Consider visiting during the winter; January and February are the least crowded. Note: As you cross the dam bridge, you also cross the state line into Arizona and into a new time zone, Mountain Time.

The Colorado River's **Black Canyon (20)** *(below Hoover Dam)*, can be explored in a motorized pontoon with a knowledgeable guide and boat full of fellow adventurers via **Black Canyon/Willow Beach River Adventures** *(Hacienda Hotel & Casino, Hwy. 93, Boulder City,*

702-294-1414 or 800-455-3490, www.blackcanyon adventures.com). The tour launches at 9:30AM below the dam; you'll return by 3PM. Wear a bathing suit, hat, and lots of sunscreen. You'll learn about the area's history and natural wonders as you attempt to spy big-horn sheep, osprey, and great blue heron in their natural settings. Rates run $82.95 for adults and $50.95 to $79.95 for kids.

TOP PICK!

Lots of Las Vegas visitors make a ★**GRAND CANYON (21)** *(South Rim entrance N. of I-40, open year-round; North Rim entrance near Hwy. 67, open May to mid-Oct., 928-638-7888, www.nps.gov/grca)* expedition part of their trip. The magnificent canyon, actually located in Arizona, cuts a swath 277 miles long, 18 miles wide, and nearly a mile deep. The canyon can be explored in a variety of ways: by driving—it's about five hours from Las Vegas to the popular South Rim entrance, and two hours by car to Grand Canyon West, home of the new Skywalk *(see next page)*. You can also see it by small-plane flyover, or by helicopter into the canyon. The city abounds with

canyon tour operators that take guests by air and land all year-round. City visitor guides, such as *What's On* magazine *(www.what's-on.com)* and *LVM (www.lasvegasmagazine.com)*, provide listings and sometimes discount coupons for these top-dollar tours. **Scenic Airlines** *(terminal located at 13 Airport Rd., Boulder*

City, 702-638-3300 or 800-634-6801, www.scenic.com, M–F 8AM–5:30PM) offers a variety of tours, including an all-day "Odyssey Tour" via a De Havilland Twin Otter Vistaliner that covers the canyon, **Hoover Dam (19)**, **Lake Mead (16)**, and more. Helicopter tours are also available to **Zion National Park (13)**. For extra-thrilling canyon views, try the Hualapai (pronounced WALL-uh-pie) tribe's new **Grand Canyon Skywalk** *(Grand Canyon West, 877-716-WEST [9378], www.destinationgrand canyon.com, www.grandcanyonskywalk.com)*, which allows visitors to walk on a suspended, U-shaped arm of glass 70 feet past the canyon's edge and 4,000 feet above its floor.

PLACES TO EAT & DRINK
Where to Eat:

The area's Station Casinos chain properties' crowd-pleasing **"Feast Buffets"** offer some of the best off-Strip buffet bang for the buck. Their **Feast Buffet at Sunset Station (23) ($)** *(1301 W. Sunset Rd. near Boulder Hwy., Henderson, 702-547-7777, www.sunsetstation.com, dinner daily 4PM–10PM)* charges $13.99 for buffet extravaganzas you build from seven "live action" international stations. **The Feast Around the World Buffet at Green Valley Ranch Resort (24) ($)** *(2300 Paseo Verde Pkwy. and I-515, Henderson, 702-617-6831, www.greenvalleyranchresort.com, 3:30PM–10PM)* charges $18.99 for a dinner that may include

Mongolian, Italian, American, Chinese, or low-carb choices. **The Feast Buffet at Red Rock Casino Resort Spa (25) ($)** *(11011 W. Charleston Blvd. just east of I-215, 702-797-7777, www.redrocklasvegas.com, daily 4PM–10PM)* offers Italian, Chinese, sushi, barbecue, and American among its food stations for $18.99. Its weekend champagne brunch is also $18.99. **Tip:** Buffet prices are discounted for those with "Boarding Pass" players cards, available free just by registering at a Station Casino. Passes also allow you to accrue points toward free buffets and other benefits when playing slots and video poker machines.

The Station Casinos present many other dining choices, too. For example, a fun place to get the day started is **The Original Pancake House (26) ($)** *(Green Valley Ranch Resort, 2300 Paseo Verde Pkwy. and I-515, Henderson, 702-617-6831, www.greenvalleyranchresort.com, 6AM–9PM)*, specializing in apple pancakes with a cinnamon glaze, and crêpes with bananas sliced in sour cream and tempered with Triple Sec, sherry, and brandy. **T-Bones Chophouse (27) ($$$)** *(Red Rock Casino Resort Spa, 11011 W. Charleston Blvd. just east of I-215, 702-797-7576, www.redrocklasvegas.com, Su–Th 5PM–10PM, F–Sa 5PM–11PM)* puts surf and turf on the table with plenty

of comfort food to complement, notably mac and cheese and garlic mashed potatoes, all enhanced by a 7,500-bottle wine loft. Dig into the Texas specialties at the **Salt Lick Bar B-Q (28) ($)** *(Red Rock Casino Resort*

Spa, 11011 W. Charleston Blvd. just east of I-215, 702-797-7576, www.redrocklasvegas.com, daily 11AM–10PM). Chow down on pulled pork, ribs of all fashions, sausage links, and more, washed down with Lone Star microbrews.

The nearby **JW Marriott Las Vegas (56)** makes a perfect stop for a fancy meal or a casual bite. **Ceres (29) ($$$)** *(JW Marriott Las Vegas, 221 N. Rampart Blvd., 702-869-7381, www.jwlasvegasresort.com, daily 6AM–2:30PM, 5PM–10PM)* offers elegance with views of waterfalls, pools, and gardens, and such treats as chicken apple soup, honey- and garlic-rubbed rack of lamb, and risotto of Oregon chanterelles. **Spiedini Ristorante (30) ($$)** *(JW Marriott Las Vegas, 221 N. Rampart Blvd., 702-869-7790, www.jwlasvegas resort.com, 5PM–10PM)*, signature of noted chef **Gustav Mauler**, serves Milanese classics, handcrafted pastas, and spit-roaster selections. Make a toast to the chef in the **Gustav Mauler Cigar Lounge (31)** *(JW Marriott Las Vegas, 221 N. Rampart Blvd., 702-869-7750, www.gustav maulercigar.com, daily 4PM–until the smoke clears)* with a Partagas, Arturo Fuente, Cohiba, or Mauler hand-rolled cigar and a martini. **Tip:** Martinis are $5 on Wednesdays.

Vintner Grill (32) ($$-$$$) *(10100 W. Charleston Blvd. at Hualupai Way, Ste. 150, 702-214-5590, www.vglas vegas.com, lunch daily 11AM–4PM, dinner Su–Th 4PM–10PM, F–Sa 4PM–11PM)* is a true find; indeed, finding it is half the challenge. But its location in Summerlin, close to the **Red Rock Casino Resort Spa (55)** and **JW Marriott Las Vegas (56)** is indicative of the city's movement west to the Spring Mountains, and its newer, up-and-coming business clusters and neighborhoods. Its retro-chic interiors, like those seen in the boutique hotels of Los Angeles and Palm Springs, have attracted such stars as Madonna, Jagger, McCartney, Springsteen, and Leno, among others. Under-30 star chef **Matthew Silverman**, a Wolfgang Puck protégé, has made his mark on this competitive culinary scene with an American-Mediterranean fusion approach; entrées might include bistro steak medallions with basmati rice, snap peas, and portabella mushroom cream, or lamb osso bucco with laurel leaf orzo and mint. Artisanal cheese tastings are big here. Lunch menus present a lighter selection and offer an option for half-orders.

Rosemary's Restaurant (33) ($$$) *(8125 W. Sahara Ave. at S. Cimarron Rd., 702-869-2251, www.rosemarys restaurant.com, lunch M–F 11:30AM–2:30PM, dinner daily 5:30PM–close)* plays like a beat from the Catherine Zeta-Jones film *No Reservations.*

Recipes and food choices from the experiences and travels of chefs **Wendy and Michael Jordan** enhance their culinary masterpieces. Expect French-fusion/Orleans–inspired offerings like apple bacon-crusted salmon and hush puppy sides. Menu items such as a Maytag blue cheese New York strip, and prosciutto-wrapped Sonoma goat cheese-stuffed figs, taste as good as they sound. A small-plates or tapas menu is also available, and the menu suggests wine pairings for each entrée. The prix-fixe dinner menu runs $50 before wine.

Bistro Zinc (34) ($-$$$) *(15 Via Bel Canto, MonteLago Village, Henderson, 702-567-ZINC [9462], www. bistrozinclv.com, lunch W–Sa, 11:30AM–5PM, dinner M–Th 5:30PM–10PM, F–Sa 5:30PM–midnight, Su 5:30PM–10PM)* is a gem. The creation of **Joseph Keller** (who, with brother Thomas, opened famed Bouchon in Yountville, CA), the restaurant offers a masterful mélange of French, American, and Orleans cuisine in a colorful, bayou-influenced space. Signature dishes include escargot Bourguignon, chicken pot pie, po boys, and Euro-style pizzas. Entrées range from $15 to

$40. The **Sunday live jazz brunch** *(11AM–3PM)* features dishes like Maine lobster, shrimp salad, and brioche French toast, accompanied by homemade popovers with Jennifer's jam.

Bars & Nightlife:

For LA-style nightlife, try **Whiskey Bar (35)** *(Green Valley Ranch Resort, 2300 Paseo Verde Pkwy., 702-617-7560, www.greenvalleyranchresort.com, Su–Th 5PM–2AM, F–Sa 6PM–3AM)*. This was Cindy Crawford spouse Rande Gerber's first foray into the Vegas club scene, and it's been a hit since its 2001 opening. The decor is stylish '70s (think mirrored wall tiles, metal sculptures, and white leather booths). There's no cover, and you don't have to flirt with the doorman to get in. Stretch out on an "opium" bed or share it with a few of your cool new friends. The dance floor offers four go-go platforms, and poles are not restricted to club-employed dancers. Overheated? Step outside to eight-acre **Whiskey Beach** and take in the starlight and the glimmering Strip skyline in the distance. **Cherry (36)** *(Red Rock Casino Resort Spa, 11011 W. Charleston Blvd., 702-797-7180, www.redrocklasvegas.com, Th–Sa 10PM–4AM)* boasts an 8,500-square-foot dance floor surrounded by VIP seating, an exterior fire-and-water-themed retreat with fire pit and pool, island bar, cabanas with curtains, and rotating day beds large enough for a *ménage à quatre*. The terrace is slightly higher than the pool, offering panoramic views of the outside action. Possibly most intriguing, however, are the men's bathrooms, with their ruby-hued, glass-lip urinals, and a one-way window wall.

Tired of desert chic? Just want a down-home good time? Try **Boulder Highway**, a country-and-western strip lined with bars and honky-tonks (hours vary). Among them are **Dylan's Dance Hall and Saloon (37)** *(4660 Boulder Hwy., 702-451-4006)*; the **Dew Drop Inn (38)** *(4200 Boulder Hwy., 702-458-3184)*; **Four Mile Bar (39)** *(3650 Boulder Hwy., 702-431-6936)*, known for its karaoke enthusiasts; **Dick's Tavern (40)** *(5890 Boulder Hwy., 702-451-8524)*, popular with bikers; **Kahootz Bar (41)** *(886 S. Boulder Hwy., 702-564-2789)*; and **The Railhead (42)** *(Boulder Station, 4111 Boulder Hwy., 702-432-7777)*, offering top live entertainment.

WHERE TO SHOP

Fashion Outlets Las Vegas (43) *(32100 Las Vegas Blvd. S., I-15 at Exit 1, Primm, 702-874-1400 or 888-424-6898, www.fashionoutletlasvegas.com, open daily 10AM–8PM)* is farther afield, about 40 miles to the south, near the California state line. This first-and-last-chance shopping center gets traffic to and from Los Angeles with its monster gas station and other reasons to stop. Find **Neiman Marcus Last Call** as well as **Burberry**, **Tahari**, and **Kenneth Cole**—more than 100 designer outlets. The excursion comes with a thrill or two for the kids: **Desperado Roller Coaster**, considered one of the world's tallest and fastest, and **Turbo Drop**, where riders can take the plunge (even if outlet prices don't).

A pleasant mall to meander to the east is the District at Green Valley Ranch Reosrt (44) *(2240 Village Walk Dr., 702-564-8595, www.thedistrictatgvr.com)*. This one, however, is pure retail rather than of the outlet variety. Connected to the Green Valley Ranch Resort (57), the complex combines loft residences and offices with an outdoor promenade and more than 70 stores and cafés. Stores range from boutiques like **PINK** and **Francesca's Collections** to **Sharper Image**, **Pottery Barn**, and **REI**.

New open-air mall **Towne Square Las Vegas** *(6605 Las Vegas Blvd., S. 702-269-5001, www.townesquarelasvegas.com)* offers shopping, dining, movies, and a kids' park/playground.

WHERE TO STAY

Visiting **Death Valley (7)**? Its Furnace Creek Inn and Furnace Creek Ranch Resort (45) *(see page 150)* make perfect winter getaways.

On **Mt. Charleston (8)**, the Hotel on Mount Charleston (46) *(see page 150)* and the Mount Charleston Lodge (47) *(see page 151)* provide cool escapes from Vegas when summer temps soar.

In **Mesquite (12)**, the CasaBlanca Resort, Casino, Golf & Spa (48) and the Oasis Resort, Casino, Golf & Spa (49) *(see page 153)* offer relaxing accommodations.

You can also get away from it all at **Lake Las Vegas (14)**, about 20 minutes from the Strip and a world away in space and pace. No neon here; you're right up against the foothills, and can even see stars at night. Stay at the Ritz-Carlton, Lake Las Vegas (50) ($$$) *(1610 Lake Las Vegas Pkwy., Henderson, 702-567-4700, www.ritz carlton.com)* with Tuscan touches, lake views, and gondolas that take guests to the village. Rooms come with goose-down duvets, oversized marble baths, and soft, thick robes. Guests may paddleboat, kayak, or canoe, stargaze with a sky connoisseur, or golf at two adjoining championship courses. Children from five through 12 can take part in "Ritz Kids" programs. The **Club Level Lounge** spoils with presentations of hors d'oeuvres, meals, and nightcap desserts. And the **Spa at the Ritz-Carlton** is a separate facility where all manner of treatments are accommodated in mansion-style surrounds.

Nearby, Loews Lake Las Vegas Resort (51) ($$$) *(101 MonteLago Blvd., Henderson, 702-567-6000 or 877-285-6397, www.loewshotels.com)*, a former Hyatt and the setting for the Julia Roberts film *America's Sweethearts*, offers romantic Moroccan ambience. Four restaurant options here, including pacific-rim inspired cuisine at **Marissa**, a 9,000-foot spa, and two championship golf courses.

MonteLago Village Resort (52) ($$-$$$) *(30 Strada di Villaggio, Henderson, 702-564-4700 or 866-564-4799, www.montelagovillage.com)* is a condo/hotel property with fashionably-furnished floor plans that range from studios to three-bedroom units. The property has a private pool area and lush landscaping that leads to lake and village. Note: There is no on-site restaurant or room service.

Join the ranks of such guests as Will Rogers, Boris Karloff, Bette Davis, Howard Hughes, and dozens of other stars, royals, and tycoons with a stay at the elegant Boulder Dam Hotel (53) *(see page 155)* near Hoover Dam (19).

The new South Point Hotel, Casino, and Spa (54) ($-$$) *(9777 Las Vegas Blvd. S. at Silverado Ranch Blvd., 702-796-7111 or 866-796-7111, www.southpointcasino. com)* is close to the Strip, but far enough away to get some room-rate advantages. Just ten minutes south of **Mandalay Bay** *(see page 140)*, the property has all the amenities of a top-tier resort, including large rooms with 42-inch plasma TVs, "Point Plush" mattresses, Wi-Fi, and free Strip shuttle service. Onsite: a 16-screen movie complex, 64-lane bowling center, an Equestrian Center, and a spa/fitness center. Its lounge and **Showroom** host DJs, events, and bands of all types, from hip-hop to rock to country to salsa. Nine dining venues (including a buffet) appeal to all appetites. Bingo is big, and rates are low.

West of town, **Red Rock Casino Resort Spa (55) ($$)** *(11011 W. Charleston Blvd., 702-797-7777 or 866-767-7773, www.redrocklasvegas.com)* corners the market on cool. A symphony in stone and crystal, the hotel offers a full-service spa with its own pool and relaxation cabanas and wonderful views of the blazing sandstone cliffs just beyond. Its **Adventure Spa** gets active guests going with mountain biking, rock climbing, hiking,

 horseback riding, and kayaking. There are ten dining venues available, quick-serve outlets like Starbucks and Ben & Jerry's, hip nightclub **Cherry (36)** *(see page 164)*, a 72-lane bowling room (the largest in Vegas, with VIP lanes offering Euro bottle services), a 16-screen cinema complex, and live entertainment. Parents like the **Kids Quest** facility, offering on-site child care from 9AM to late night.

JW Marriott Las Vegas (56) ($$$) *(221 N. Rampart Blvd. and E. Summerlin Pkwy., 702-869-7777 or 877-869-7777, www.jwlasvegasresort.com)* combines the Vegas experience with mountain views, great golf, and the marvelous expanse of the desert. Andalusian élan is exuded via fountains, pools, and villa ambience.

Luxurious rooms include expansive marble baths. The **Aquae Sulis Spa** here extends over two floors, offers indoor and outdoor relaxation areas and a list of elixirs and treatments that read like the menu from a forbidden sweets shop. Its unique hydrotherapy pools offer focused water jet systems to invigorate and relax different areas of the body. The PGA Tour **TPC Golf Club** at The Canyons down the road is accessible to guests; the hotel golf concierge can set tee times.

Green Valley Ranch Resort (57) ($$-$$$) *(2300 Paseo Verde Pkwy./Green Valley Pkwy. S. at I-215, 702-617-7777 or 866-782-9487, www.greenvalleyranch resort.com)* lies within the valley's sprawl of new-build communities. But there are reasons why it may be the resort of choice. Its rooms have a European look with regal leather furnishings, wrought-iron details, linens with high thread counts, plush robes, and private terraces on which to peruse your complimentary newspaper and sip your room-brewed coffee. The spa swimming pool has an unusual feature: a bottom window that serves as a watery "skylight" for those enjoying cinnamon facials or green tea wraps in the treatment rooms below. Diners may choose from nine restaurants and seven quick-serve spots. The street-chic District at Green Valley Ranch Resort (44) *(see page 165)* is a shoppers' paradise. Bathers go for the eight-acre designer pool area; **The Pond** is the first stop for those wishing to do away with annoying tan lines. Concerts are held at **Ovation**, an intimate space that hosts such names as Macy Gray.

INDEX

NOTES

NOTES

NOTES

NOTES

NOTES

NOTES

NOTES

NOTES